Disclaimer

The information included in this book is designed to provide helpful information on the subjects discussed. This book is not meant to be used to diagnose or treat any medical condition. For diagnosis or treatment of any medical problem, consult your own doctor. The author and publisher are not responsible for any specific health or allergy needs that may require medical supervision and are not liable for any damages or negative consequences from any application, action, treatment or preparation, to anyone reading or following the information in this book. Links may change and any references included are provided for informational purposes only.

Cooking with Spices and Herbs

100 Savory Cookbook Recipes Featuring the Best Spices and Herbs from Around the World

By Susan Hollister

Copyright © 2019

Table of Contents

CHAPTER 3: UNIQUE AND BOLD HERBS AND SPICES 45

CHAPTER 4: EXOTIC HERBS AND SPICES 61

CHAPTER 5: DELIGHTFUL CITRUS FLAVORED HERBS AND SPICES 83

CHAPTER 6: HOT AND FIERY HERBS AND SPICES 100

CHAPTER 7: SWEET AND SPICY HERBS AND SPICES 114

CONCLUSION 134

MY OTHER BOOKS 135

Introduction

Congratulations, you have made a great decision in purchasing this recipe book! In the following pages you will discover how to make 100 delicious meals, snacks and desserts using the best herbs and spices from around the world. Everyone is sure to love all the wonderful and exotic meals you will now be able to easily serve to them!

Make meal times fun again with the wide variety of new recipes and flavors that you will soon discover. If you are tired of the same old meals over and over, then this is the recipe book for you! Meals like Rosemary and Thyme Encrusted Lamb Chops will tickle your taste buds and leave you craving for more! The recipes are easy to make and easy to follow. I have researched the best combinations of spices and herbs to enhance the flavors of your meals.

Travel around the world with recipes like Festive Moroccan Couscous or try a Japanese watermelon and shiso salad. Have fun making Jamaican Jerk Chicken Legs or Creamy Mexican Tortilla Soup. Pork Loin Stuffed with Cabbage and Mushrooms with

Winter Savory is a fan favorite and Light and Fluffy Vanilla Scones will melt in your mouth.

I believe herbs and spices to be miracles, because they not only flavor food, but they also heal and have a wide variety of incredible benefits depending on which herb or spice you are using. The monks in the Middle Ages grew extensive herb gardens and the Chinese have been using herbs and spices as remedies for thousands of years. It's always nice when you can enjoy delicious and flavorful meals while helping yourself to heal all naturally.

If you would like detailed information about the descriptions, history, growing tips and health benefits of each herb or spice featured in this recipe book, just check out my companion book to this one titled: Herbs and Spices: The Top 100 Best Herbs and Spices from Around the World by Susan Hollister.

Now get excited, because you are about to discover some of your new favorite recipes filled with incredible taste sensations that you have never experienced before!

Chapter 1: Mediterranean Herbs and Spices

Many of the following recipes are from the Mediterranean where these herbs and spices originated. You will find recipes from Italy, Greece, France and more in this chapter and they all are delightfully tasty, fresh and some even help reverse indigestion and bloated feeling.

Perfect Pesto Chicken with Provolone

Featuring: Basil

Originally used as an antibiotic in Ancient Rome and Greece, Basil has a lovely spicy flavor that often helps with excess acid and gas in the stomach due to eating acidic foods like tomatoes or cheese. Therefore, basil is the perfect herb to add to spaghetti sauce. This recipe does not have tomatoes, but it does have prosciutto and cheese and they can cause some gas issues in the bowels. Basil is traditionally used in pesto and it goes quite well with chicken covered in provolone.

Ingredients:
4 boneless, skinless chicken breasts
salt and pepper to taste
1 tablespoon unsalted butter
8 large basil leaves
4 slices prosciutto
4 slices provolone

Directions:

- Melt the butter in a large skillet over medium heat.

- While the butter melts, sprinkle both sides of the chicken breasts with salt and pepper.

- Place the breasts in the pan and sauté on both sides until brown on the outside and white on the inside.

- Spray a baking dish with butter flavored non-stick spray and place the chicken breasts in.

- Top each breast with 2 basil leaves, 1 slice prosciutto and 1 slice of Provolone.

- Broil about 6 to 8 inches away from the heat for 1 to 2 minutes or until the cheese melts.

- Remove from the oven and serve.

Warm and Filling Great Northern Bean and Bay Soup

Featuring: Bay

Never eat a bay leaf, only use it as flavoring and discard the leaf when done. Bay leaves are very tough and can cause blockage in the digestive system, but their flavor is not to be missed. Bay leaves give special savory flavor to soups and stews that would be horribly missed if you didn't use them. This is a tasty soup to serve on a cold winter night. It is very savory and satisfying. It makes about 4 large servings.

Ingredients:
1 tablespoon olive oil
1 medium onion, peeled and chopped
4 cloves garlic, peeled and minced
2 carrots, peeled and chopped
1 stalk celery, chopped
4 cups vegetable broth
1 large potato, peeled and chopped
2 bay leaves
1 tablespoon dry basil
1 teaspoon sea salt
½ teaspoon ground black pepper
1/8 teaspoon dried thyme
2 15-ounce cans Great Northern Beans, drained and rinsed

Directions:

- Heat a large Dutch Oven over medium heat and add the olive oil.

- Sauté the onion for about 3 minutes and add the garlic and sauté another 2 minutes or until the onion becomes translucent.

- Add the carrot and celery and sauté another 4 minutes.

- Pour in the broth and reduce the heat to a simmer.

- Add the potato, bay leaves, salt, pepper and thyme and stir.

- Bring to a boil and reduce to a simmer for 20 minutes.

- Stir in the beans and heat through about 10 more minutes.

- Remove the bay leaves and serve.

Tasty Garlic Beer Bread

Featuring: Garlic

Garlic is a very healthy and important ingredient. I live in a town where the people are primarily Italian and Greek, so garlic is in every grocery store in every form you can imagine. I like to use whole cloves and either mince or put them through a press once I remove the papery covering on each clove. Cloves bundle together to make a head of garlic and I grow garlic in my garden. In late fall, almost when it is time for the snow to fly, the leaves are brown and dry while the heads are still attached. I braid the dry material and hang it in my root cellar to dry all the way and I usually have garlic all year round. This bread team's garlic up with some beer and makes a very tasty loaf of bread.

Ingredients:
3 cups whole wheat flour
4 cloves garlic, peeled and minced
3 tablespoons sugar
1 tablespoons baking powder
1 teaspoon salt
1 teaspoon dried rosemary

1 teaspoon dried thyme
1 teaspoon dried oregano
1 12-ounce bottle beer
4 tablespoons butter, melted

Directions

- Grease a 9 x 5 x 3-inch loaf pan

- In a large bowl whisk the flour, garlic, sugar, baking powder, salt, rosemary, thyme and oregano until well blended.

- Pour in beer and whisk gently (it will foam) until just combined.

- Mix in half the melted butter.

- Pour the rest of the butter in the bottom of the loaf pan and brush it evenly from one end to the other.

- Pour the batter in the pan and spread out evenly

- Bake in a preheated 400 degree oven for 50 to 60 minutes. Let cool at least 10 to 15 minutes before turning out of the pan and wait a few more minutes before slicing and serving.

Greek Chicken with Rigani

Featuring: Greek Oregano

Greek Oregano is different than regular, or Italian, oregano. It has a spicery and stronger flavor and goes well with the strong flavorings of Greece. It does help with digestion too and I use it in an infusion to wash down my shower every once in a while, to deter mildew from forming. The following recipe is a Greek chicken recipe that uses Greek oregano but it calls it the old name of Rigani.

Ingredients:
1 whole chicken (about 4 pounds)
1 lemon
4 tablespoons Greek oregano, divided

1 clove garlic, peeled and crushed
2 tablespoons butter, melted
3 tablespoons olive oil
salt and pepper to taste.

Directions:

- Place the chicken in a roasting pan that has been sprayed with non-stick butter flavored spray.

- Zest the lemon onto a square of wax paper and set aside and cut the lemon in half removing any visible seeds.

- Squeeze half the lemon into a small bowl and add 3 tablespoons of the Greek oregano. Pour this into the cavity of the chicken and rub around so it coats all sides.

- Squeeze the other half of the lemon into another small bowl and add lemon zest, garlic, melted butter and olive oil. Whisk well and rub this on the outside of the chicken.

- Sprinkle the chicken with the rest of the Greek oregano and the salt and pepper.

- Place the two lemon rinds inside the cavity of the chicken.

- Place in a preheated 375 degree oven for 20 minutes per pound. Remove from oven and let rest at least 10 minutes before carving. Serve with pan juices over top.

Spicy Fennel with Pasta and Greens

Featuring: Fennel

The leaves and flowers of fennel are very wispy and pretty and the seeds are delicious to chew on to get rid of bad breath. I know a few people that chew on fennel seeds to keep their mother from knowing they had an alcoholic drink, but she usually knows because that is the only reason that they chew on fennel seeds. The underground bulb is especially delicious too and has a fresh anise flavor that goes very well with pasta and greens. Use any pasta you like to make this dish, but I prefer using linguini. It makes 3 to 4 servings.

Ingredients:

1 tablespoon + ½ teaspoon olive oil, divided
1/3 cup onion, peeled and sliced thin
1/3 cup fennel, sliced thin
2 cloves garlic, peeled and crushed
1 pinch salt
1 pinch pepper
1 teaspoon balsamic vinegar
4 fresh sage leaves, chopped
8 ounces pasta, cooked and drained reserving ½ cup of cooking water
8 leaves of Swiss Chard (substitute ¾ cup to 1 cup fresh spinach)
1 lemon, juiced
¼ cup toasted walnuts (or pecans)
Parmesan cheese

Directions:

- Heat 1 tablespoon oil in a large skillet over medium high heat and add the onion, fennel and garlic with salt and pepper. Sauté until fennel is brown around the edges, about 8 to 10 minutes.

- Add the balsamic vinegar and sauté another 2 minutes or until fennel is soft. Reduce the heat and add the rest of the oil to prevent onions from burning.

- Add the sage leaves, ¼ cup of the pasta water and pasta and sauté about 4 minutes stirring constantly. Add chard and sauté another 2 to 3 minutes or until the chard wilts and becomes hot.

- Remove from heat and squeeze lemon juice over top and stir. If it seems dry or thick, add the other ¼ cup of pasta water (or more).

- Squeeze lemon over top, add the walnuts and Parmesan and toss.

- Serve immediately.

14

Sweet and Crunchy Lavender Honey Biscotti

Featuring: Lavender

Lavender is my favorite herb and mostly because it is so useful. The scent is amazing and it gets rid of insects. I put dried lavender flowers in sachets and put them with my stored winter sweaters in the summer. They come out smelling sweet when I need them and no holes from moths. I love to make lavender wreaths from fresh stemmed lavender and hanging them to dry. The scent the house with an amazing perfume. Some would say that using lavender in food makes the food taste soapy and I say that is because they used too much lavender. Lavender combines well with baked goods and it is the herb mix of Bouquet Garni that is wonderful with roast beef and poultry. This biscotti is truly delicious and it makes about 3 dozen biscotti. If you burn yourself taking it out of the oven, put some lavender oil and the burn and it will not blister and will heal quicker than normal.

Ingredients:
2 ¼ cup all-purpose flour
1 teaspoon baking powder
½ teaspoon baking soda
¼ teaspoon salt
2/3 cup granulated sugar
3 eggs
3 tablespoons honey
½ teaspoon vanilla
2 tablespoons orange zest
1 teaspoon dried lavender flowers

Directions:

- Preheat the oven to 350 degrees Fahrenheit and place rack in the middle. Grease 3 baking sheets with and cover with parchment paper.

- Measure the flour, baking powder, baking soda and salt and whisk well.

- In another bowl combine the sugar with the eggs and whisk until frothy. Add the honey, vanilla, orange zest and lavender and mix until well combined.

- Add the dry ingredients gradually to the wet ingredients using a wooden spoon at first and then the hands. It should form a sticky bread-like dough.

- Place wax paper on a flat surface and sprinkle with flour. Cut the dough in 6 equal pieces and on the wax paper, form 6 loaves about 3-inches wide, 7-inches long and 3/4-inch high. Place 2 loaves on each sheet about 3 to 4 inches apart.

- Bake each sheet separately about 25 minutes reversing the sheets front to back after 10 minutes of baking. The loaves should not be brown after cooking. Take out of the oven and let rest 10 minutes.

- Reduce oven to 275 degrees.

- Cut into slices with a sharp, serrated knife about ½ inch thick and place back on baking sheets. Bake 15 more minutes.

- Cool completely and, if desired, drizzle with a powder sugar, water and vanilla glaze. I tint mine with a little bit of purple food coloring to make it lavender. Store in airtight containers.

Rustic Chicken with Marjoram and Tomatoes

Featuring: Marjoram

If you get food poisoning, the best thing you can do is drink some marjoram tea. It eases the pain in the stomach and gets rid of toxins. The following recipe is a rustic Mediterranean recipe using chicken breasts tomatoes, garlic and marjoram. I use coconut oil because of health benefits but you can also use olive oil only reduce it to 1/8 cup.

Ingredients:
4 cups cherry tomatoes, stemmed and cut in half
¼ cup coconut oil, melted

4 cloves garlic, peeled and crushed in garlic press
1 ¼ teaspoon red pepper flakes, crushed
2 tablespoon fresh marjoram, chopped, divided
4 chicken breast halves, with ribs
salt and pepper to taste

Directions:

- Preheat the oven to 450 degrees Fahrenheit.

- In a bowl, place the halved cherry tomatoes, coconut oil, garlic, red pepper flakes and 1 tablespoon of the marjoram and toss to coat.

- Place the chicken on a rimmed cooking sheet that has been sprayed with non-stick spray. Sprinkle the breasts with salt and pepper.

- Pour the tomato mixture on top of the chicken and arrange on and round the breasts.

- Roast 35 minutes until the tomatoes blister and chicken cooks through.

- Transfer the chicken to a serving plate and spoon the tomatoes and juice over top.

- Sprinkle with the rest of the marjoram and serve.

New York Style Pizza Sauce with Oregano and Herbs

Featuring: Oregano

Regular oregano is easy to find dried and fresh in the grocery store and it is traditionally cooked in Italian dishes. Pizza is a regular dinner at my house and this sauce is very good. I make the sauce a head of time, put it in a mason jar or freezer bag and either keep it in the refrigerator a few days or freezer a few months and any time I feel like pizza, it comes out and goes on the crust.

Ingredients:

1 4.5 ounce can diced tomatoes with juice
1 6 ounce can tomato paste
1 ½ tablespoon olive oil
2 tablespoons fresh basil leaves, chopped
1 ½ teaspoon dry oregano
1 teaspoon granulated sugar
 1 clove garlic, peeled and minced
1 teaspoon Kosher salt

Directions:

- Combine the tomatoes with juice, tomato paste, olive oil, basil, oregano, sugar, garlic and salt in a medium size bowl. Use a whisk so all is combined.

- Spread on pizza crust or put in airtight container in the refrigerators about 5 days or freeze in a freezer bag for about 2 months.

- When ready to use, bring to room temperature first.

Lemon Parsley Potato Side Dish

Featuring: Parsley

Parsley is another common herb from the Mediterranean that grows easily in your back yard garden. I use Italian flat leaf parsley for cooking because the curly leaf is not nearly as flavorful. Eat it cooked or sprinkled on without cooking and it will make your dishes not only taste good but look good. Parsley had an extraordinary amount of Vitamin C in it and I think I rarely get a cold just because the amount of parsley I consume. Parsley pares well with potatoes and when you add lemon too, it makes a scrumptious side dish making about 10 servings. I serve this side dish with ham or lamb at Easter and periodically throughout the year with any meat.

Ingredients:

3 pounds red potatoes, skin on, quartered

½ cup butter, melted
3 tablespoons fresh lemon juice
3 tablespoons fresh parsley, minced

Directions:

- Cook the potatoes in boiling water until they are tender, about 15 minutes and drain.

- In a saucepan, melt the butter and add the lemon juice and parsley, whisking it in.

- Place the potatoes in a serving dish and pour the butter mixture over top, tossing lightly.

- Serve while warm.

Rosemary and Thyme Encrusted Lamb Chops

Featuring: Rosemary

Rosemary's thin evergreen-like leaves pack in a lot of flavor. Rosemary oil keeps you in concentration mode, so I put it in a water infuser when I write. It seems to do the trick. I also use it in dishes frequently because it does tend to help the immune system stay strong. Rosemary goes great with fish, poultry, beef, and really goes well with lamb chops. This recipe makes 4 chops.

Ingredients:
8 lamb chops (about 3 ounce ones)
½ teaspoon ground black pepper
¼ teaspoon Kosher salt
3 tablespoons Dijon mustard
1 tablespoon fresh rosemary, minced
1 tablespoon fresh thyme, minced
3 cloves garlic, peeled and minced

Directions:

- Sprinkle the chops on both sides with pepper and salt.

- In a bowl, combine the Dijon, rosemary, thyme and garlic in a bowl and set aside.

- Grill the chops in an oiled rack over medium covered with foil for about 6 minutes and turn.

- Spread the herb mixture on the chops and grill 6 to 8 more minutes or until the internal temperature of the chops is about 140 degrees Fahrenheit.

- Serve warm.

Old Time Sage Bread Stuffing Recipe

Featuring: Sage

I used to put chicken wire around my sage and fill it with dried tree leaves once the weather got cold. The sage would keep growing all the way to Thanksgiving, so I would have fresh sage leaves to put in my turkey stuffing. The following recipe is my mother's sage bread stuffing and it is good for a 15 to 20 pound turkey. Make half for stuff porkchops. I used to put it in the turkey, but now I put it in a big pan and it makes about 12 servings. We would cut all the bread in cubes and place it on baking sheets to dry overnight.

Ingredients:
1 ½ cups (3 stalks) celery, chopped
1 cup (1 large) onion, peeled and chopped
½ cup butter
1 tablespoon fresh sage, chopped or 1 teaspoon dried, ground sage
¼ teaspoon ground black pepper
¼ teaspoon salt
12 cups dried breadcrumbs
1 to 1 ¼ cup chicken broth
extra sage leaves, if using fresh

Directions:
- Preheat the oven to 325 degrees Fahrenheit.

- Chop the celery and onions and set aside.

- Melt the butter in a large skillet over medium heat. Once melted add the celery and onion and sauté until they are crisp tender and remove from heat.

- Stir in the sage, pepper and salt and set aside.

- Place the breadcrumbs in a large bowl and pour the butter mixture over top. Mix with a big wooden spoon and add enough chicken broth to make it a moist mixture that slightly holds together when pressed between hands (like making a snowball).

- Pour into a non-stick sprayed 2 quart baking dish, cover with foil and bake 30 minutes.

- Remove foil and bake another 10 minutes so the stuffing gets a little crunchy on the top and sprinkle on whole fresh leaves before serving.

NOTE: If you want to stuff a turkey, wait until right before cooking the turkey to make   the stuffing in a large bowl and only use ¾ cup to 1 cup chicken broth.

Sautéed Thyme Flavored Zucchini

Featuring: Thyme

Thyme has a little tiny leaf that is a miracle because of all it can do. The thymol in the leaf is antibiotic, anti-inflammatory and anti-fungal and is often used to get rid of infections. That said, the little leaves have a lovely flavor that goes with meats and vegetables very well. The following recipe is a side dish to serve with roast is treated with thyme when cooking. It uses the prolific zucchini in a very delicious manner.

Ingredients:
1 tablespoon olive oil
1 clove garlic, peeled and minced
¼ cup onion, peeled and chopped fine

1 pound zucchini, quartered lengthwise and halved (leave skin on)
1 teaspoon fresh thyme, chopped
2 tablespoons fresh parsley, chopped
¼ teaspoon red pepper flakes, crushed

Directions:

- Place a large skillet over medium high heat and add the oil.

- Sauté the garlic and onions for about 2 minutes or until fragrant.

- Add the zucchini and thyme and sauté 4 to 5 minutes until tender crisp.

- Sprinkle parsley and red pepper flakes over top and stir while warming.

- Serve immediately as a side dish.

In chapter two you will learn about herbs and spices that have an earthy flavor profile
and give special flavor to main dishes, desserts, sandwiches and side dishes.

Chapter 2: Earthy Essential Herbs and Spices

Earthy herbs are those that might taste like grasses, hay or actual soil. Onions might be hot, but they also an earthy flavor. Poppyseed has an earthy taste that is mild and crunchy. Sometimes they taste like things other than herbs and spices. Borage tastes like cucumber and chamomile like apples. The flavors of these herbs are always in the background and make dishes taste better than if they were not there.

Cream Cheese and Borage Sandwich Spread

Featuring: Borage

The cucumber flavor of borage blooms and leaves makes for a nice cream cheese sandwich spread. I make little tea sandwiches when I need a lift in my spirits because borage does improve your mood if not just from the flavor. Try some borage tea along with them for a real boost.

Ingredients:
1 – 8 ounce block of cream cheese, softened
1 tablespoon milk
½ teaspoon garlic salt
2 tablespoons chopped borage leaves
¼ cup sweet red bell pepper, seeded and chopped fine
mini bread or dense bread with crust removed
borage leaves and flowers (remove the orange or yellow septal)

Directions:

- In a food processor, combine the cream cheese, milk, garlic salt, chopped borage leaves and red pepper. Pulse lightly. Do not process so smooth you cannot see the red pepper or leaves; just enough to combine them. (I just mix with a fork sometimes).

- Spread on mini bread and leave open face or spread on crustless bread and cut into halves or fourths and leave open face.

- Garnish with borage leaves and flowers.

- Refrigerate covered until ready to serve. Do not leave in the refrigerator more than 2 to 3 hours.

Buttery Chamomile Cookies

Featuring: Chamomile

Chamomile does have the faint flavor of apples and the recipe I chose for this herb is a delicious buttery cookie that has that slight taste of apple. The cookies don't need to be chewed because they just melt with the flavor of chamomile. This recipe makes about 18 cookies and there are no eggs in the ingredients. Store them in an airtight container if you can keep them around longer than a few minutes.

Ingredients:
1 cup unsalted butter
¼ teaspoons salt
½ cup granulated sugar
The zest of 1 lemon
1 teaspoon dried and ground chamomile flowers
2 ¼ cup all-purpose flour

Directions:
- Preheat the oven to 325 degrees F.

- In a mixing bowl with a mixer, beat the butter, salt and sugar until it is light and fluffy.

- Slowly blend in the lemon zest and chamomile flowers. Add the flour, a little at a time until it is all incorporated. This makes a thick batter.

- Press the dough into an 8-inch square pan that has been sprayed with non-stick spray.

- Bake for 30 minutes until the cookies are golden. While still warm, cut squares, but let cool in the pan on a rack.

Chicken With Creamy Chervil Sauce

Featuring: Chervil

Chervil has a mild flavor and is used in French recipes. The herb gets rid of excess liquid in the body and relieve an upset stomach. The sauce for this dish is mild and delightful and will please anyone who loves French cuisine. It makes 4 servings.

Ingredients:
2 teaspoons unsalted butter
3 tablespoons green onion or shallot, chopped
4 boneless skinless chicken breasts
1 ¼ cup chicken stock
1 large bunch (3 tablespoons) chervil
Kosher salt and ground pepper to taste
2 tablespoons cornstarch

Directions:
- Melt the butter in a large frying pan over low heat and add the onion. Cook for about 3 minutes stirring or until the onion softens.

- Place the chicken in the pan and cook on both sides until just brown.

- Add the stock and cover the pan simmering for about 8 minutes.

- Turn the chicken and add the chervil simmering another 4 minutes. Remove the chicken to a plate and keep warm.

- Season the sauce with salt and pepper.

- Mix the cornstarch into the sauce, whisking well and bring the sauce to a boil. Keep whisking.

- Immediately lower the heat to a simmer and whisk while cooking 2 more minutes while the sauce gets thick.

- Serve the chicken with sauce poured over top. Garnish with a little more fresh-chopped chervil.

Herb and Chia Seed Encrusted Sweet Potato Wedges

Featuring: Chia Seeds

Not only are the following cheese wedges delicious, but they have a nice crunch to them due to the chia seed. They are super easy to make either in the oven or in your air fryer. The recipe calls for chia oil but you can also use vegetables oil and if you do use your air fryer only use 1 tablespoon of the oil mixing it with the other ingredients and then coating the potatoes with it. This recipe makes about 6 wedges.

Ingredients:
3 medium sweet potatoes, skinned and cut in wedges
½ teaspoon smoked paprika
1 ½ teaspoon chia seeds
¼ cup grated Parmesan cheese
½ teaspoon dried parsley flakes
1 ½ tablespoon chia oil

Directions:
- Peel and slice the potato wedges and set aside.

- In a small bowl combine the paprika, chia seeds, Parmesan and parsley using a whisk to mix it up well.

- Place the potato wedges in a bowl and pour over the oil. Toss to coat.

- Sprinkle in the seasoning mix and again, toss to coat.

- Put them in an air fryer to cook for 12 minutes, turning once at 400 degrees F, or place foil on a baking pan with sides, spray with non-stick spray and put the wedges on so they don't touch and bake in a 400 degree F oven for 20 minutes turning halfway through.

Creamy Cilantro Lime Chicken

Featuring: Cilantro

Cilantro is most often used in Latin inspired dishes and has a nice mild flavor. It expels toxins from the body and also is good for the brain and anxiety. This cilantro chicken dish is a bit sassy and saucy and is great for family or guests. It will serve 4 people.

Ingredients:
4 medium boneless, skinless chicken breasts
salt and pepper to taste
1 tablespoons olive oil
¼ cup onion, peeled and chopped
2 cloves garlic, peeled and minced
1 cup chicken broth
1 lime, squeezed using the juice only
½ teaspoon red pepper flakes, crushed
½ cup heavy cream
2 tablespoons fresh cilantro, chopped

Directions:
- Season the chicken breasts on both sides with salt and pepper and set aside.

- Heat a skillet over medium heat and add the olive oil.

- Add the onion to the skillet and sauté about 3 minutes.

- Add the garlic to the skillet and sauté 2 minutes or until the garlic becomes fragrant and onion becomes translucent. Do not let them brown.

- Place the chicken breasts in the skillet and sauté about 4 minutes, turning and another 4 to 5 minutes on the other side until done. Remove to a plate and cover with foil to keep warm.

- Add the chicken broth, lime juice, and red pepper flakes. Add more salt and pepper if desired. Bring to a low boil and let simmer 8 minutes or until the liquid reduces to ¼ cup.

- Bring heat up and let boil. When it comes to a boil, add the cream and turn the burner off. Whisk well.

- Add the chicken back to the skillet and cover to let sit about 2 minutes with a lid on.

- Sprinkle with cilantro and serve.

Chicken and Mushrooms with Earthy Dill Sauce

Featuring: Dill

Mushrooms and dill go well together because they both have an earthy flavor. Dill is often used to make pickles but it is so much more than that. It works good for digestive issues and supplies your intestines with good bacteria. This chicken recipe is simply lovely and the dill flavor permeates the chicken. If you like dill flavoring, you will love this dish.

Ingredients:
1 tablespoon olive oil
½ teaspoon salt
¼ teaspoon pepper
1 pound boneless, skinless chicken thighs, cut in 1-inch cubes
1 medium onion, peeled and chopped
1 teaspoon garlic, peeled and chopped (about 2 cloves)
12 ounces mushrooms, cleaned and cut in half
½ cup white dry wine
1 cup chicken broth
2 tablespoons fresh dill, chopped fine
½ cup sour cream
2 tablespoons unsalted butter at room temperature

1 tablespoon flour

Directions:

- Heat a skillet over medium heat and add the oil.

- Salt and pepper the chicken thigh cubes and set aside.

- Place the onion and garlic in the pan and sauté about 2 minutes or until the onion is soft.

- Add the chicken and brown on both sides cooking about 5 to 7 minutes or until the chicken is cooked through with no pink showing.

- Add the mushrooms and stir. Cook about 5 more minutes.

- Pour in the wine and broth and bring to a boil. Sprinkle in the dill and stir in the sour cream.

- Remove the chicken with a slotted spoon to a serving plate and cover with foil to keep warm.

- Add the butter and stir to melt.

- Ladle some of the bubbling sauce into a bowl and sprinkle in the flour. Whisk well and pour it back in the skillet whisking constantly over a simmer until the sauce thickens about 5 minutes.

- Pour the chicken back in and get warm and serve over mashed potatoes, rice or pasta.

Chewy Breakfast Cookies with Flax and Dried Fruit

Featuring: Flax

Breakfast cookies are so easy because you can just grab one as you go out the door to the bus or car. Flax is very healthy for your body supplying it with fiber. This recipe makes 12 huge cookies that are made in a muffin tin (that is how big they are). They have no flour, no oil and no egg and my vegan friends love them.

Ingredients:

2/3 cup flaxseed meal
½ cup unsweetened almond or peanut butter
1/3 cup real maple syrup, honey or agave nectar
½ cup unsweetened dairy-free milk (I use almond milk)
1 teaspoon vanilla
1 teaspoon ground cinnamon
2/3 cup dried fruit (raisins, cranberries, blueberries apricots)

Directions:

- Preheat oven to 325 degrees Fahrenheit and spray 12 muffin cups in a tin with non-stick spray.

- In a large bowl, combine the flaxseed meal, nut butter, chosen sweetener, milk, vanilla and cinnamon and use a wooden spoon to mix it up.

- Once well mixed, add the dried fruit and fold it in evenly.

- Spoon the batter evenly into the 12 prepared muffin cups and bake 25 to 30 minutes and the edges are brown and tops look dry.

- Place tin on wire rack and cool 5 minutes.

- Turn out onto the wire rack by turning upside down and tapping on the cups. They should just plop out onto the rack. Let cool before eating or they will fall apart.

- Store cookies in an airtight container up to 5 days or wrap each cookie well in plastic wrap, place in a freezer bag and freeze 6 months. Take out of the freezer the night before and let come to room temperature.

Roast Pork with Juniper Berries

Featuring: Juniper Berry

Truthfully, juniper berries have a flavor that many people do not like, but they are tasty once you get used to them. They are very good for the urinary tract and I always make something with them if I get a urinary tract infection (or I drink the tea from dried berries). The following recipe is great to serve any time but is very impressive and great for when you have dinner guests because the flavor is so unusual.

Ingredients:
3 tablespoons olive oil
2 ounces pancetta, minced
1 pound pork tenderloin
salt and pepper to taste
1 tablespoon juniper berries
4 sprigs fresh rosemary
3 sprigs fresh thyme
3 bay leaves
2 cloves garlic, peeled and minced
1 cup dry white wine
1 cup chicken stock

Directions:

- Place a Dutch oven over medium high heat and let it warm up. Pour in the oil.

- Cook the pancetta, stirring constantly, about 2 to 3 minutes and remove with a slotted spoon to a plate covered with a paper towel.

- Season the tenderloin with salt and pepper and place in the skillet. Brown well on all sides.

- Add the juniper berries, rosemary, thyme, bay leaves and garlic and cook 1 to 2 minutes.

- Pour in the wine and scrape the brown bits from the bottom. Simmer about 10 minutes watching so the pan doesn't dry out. `

- Add the stock and bring to a boil. Bring heat to a simmer, partially cover and cook 15 to 30 minutes until an instant thermometer inserted into the pork reads 145 degrees F.

- Turn off the heat and let rest at least 5 minutes. Remove the meat to a cutting board and slice.

- Turn the heat up on the sauce and bring to a simmer. Let simmer about 10 minutes or until it gets thick. Remove the bay leaves, berries and sprigs of herbs.

- Pour the sauce over top the pork and serve.

Incredible Potato Lovage Soup

Featuring: Lovage

Lovage is good for just about anything that might ail you. It works with coughs and colds, heals skin problems, and more but it also has a very nice earthy flavor. Potato Lovage soup is a real treat on a cold night because it warms the body and the soul. The recipe makes 4 large servings.

Ingredients:
2 tablespoons butter
1 medium onion, peeled and chopped
2 ½ pounds potatoes, peeled and cut in chunks
1 quart chicken or vegetable stock
1 ounce lovage leaves, without the stems
3 cups milk
½ teaspoon salt
½ teaspoon ground black pepper
1 teaspoon lovage seed

Directions:
- Melt butter in a stock pot and sauté the onion in it for about 8 minutes, stirring frequently.

- Add the potato and chicken stock and bring to a boil. Immediately reduce to a simmer and cover for 20 minutes.

- Add the lovage leaves and simmer 5 more minutes.

- Turn off the heat and let cool 10 minutes.

- Add the milk, salt and pepper and use an immersion blender or put batches in a regular blender to blend.

- Warm it up a little on the stove and ladle into bowls. Sprinkle on more chopped lovage leaves and seeds.

- This soup can also be served as a cold soup.

French Onion Soup with Baguette and Melted Gruyere Cheese Topping

Featuring: Onion

French Onion Soup is the most delicious and cheesy soup I have ever eaten. I do use a milder onion to make mine but the flavor still comes roaring through. Here is a hint: After chopping onions your hands will often smell and no amount of washing will get that smell off. Take an old silver spoon and run it over your hands. The smell will be gone. This soup has a slice of bread (baguette) that floats on top with melted cheese over top. It is so cheese and good you will not be able to stop at one bowl.

Ingredients:
½ cup unsalted butter
4 sweet to medium hot onions, peeled and sliced thin
2 cloves garlic, peeled and chopped
2 bay leaves
2 springs of thyme or 1 teaspoon dried thyme
Kosher salt and ground pepper to taste
1 cup red wine
3 heaping tablespoons all-purpose flour
2 quarts beef broth
1 baguette sliced
½ pound Gruyere cheese, grated

Directions:

- Melt the butter in a large stock pot over medium heat.

- Sauté the onions, garlic about 5 minutes or until soft and add the bay leaves, thyme, salt and pepper. Cook until onions are browned and caramelized, stirring frequently, about 20 minutes.
- Add the wine and bring to a boil. Immediately reduce to a simmer and simmer 5 minutes.
- Remove the bay leaves and thyme sprig and discard.
- Evenly sprinkle with the flour and stir in. Turn to medium low heat and simmer 10 minutes making sure the flour does not go to the bottom of the pan and burn. I like to use a whisk.
- Add the broth and simmer another 10 minutes. Check after to see if the salt and pepper is good for your taste and adjust.
- When ready to serve, heat up the broiler to high. Arrange the baguette slices on a broiler tray or baking sheet and toast.
- Ladle soup into heat resistant bowls that can go in the broiler. Place a toasted slice of bread on top and then sprinkle evenly with the cheese. Broil 3 to 5 minutes or until the cheese is bubbly and lightly browned.
- Serve immediately.

Sautéed Savory Plantain with Butter and Garlic

Featuring: Plantain

The plantain herb described here is a green plant with a long stem and green bumpy flowers at the end. You may see plantain growing in the grass and rabbits love it. It is the leaves that are used to flavor this dish and they taste slightly like mild asparagus and when cooked in garlic and butter, it makes a stupendous side dish for 4.

Ingredients:
2 tablespoons unsalted butter
2 small green onions, chopped
1 clove garlic, peeled and minced
2 cups plantain leaves, washed, dried and chopped lightly

Salt and pepper to taste

Directions:

- Melt the butter in a skillet over medium heat.

- Add the onion and garlic and sauté about 2 minutes.

- Add the plantain and sauté until wilted, dark green and heated through.

- Season with salt and pepper and add a squirt of apple cider vinegar if desired.

- Serve hot.

Deliciously Sweet Lemon Poppy Seed Sweet Bread

Featuring: Poppy Seed

Poppy seed is delightfully earthy and crunchy and are great for providing the body with fiber. This makes the seed good for any digestive issues. The following recipe is for a delicious bread that doesn't really taste like bread but a lovely cake. This recipe makes 2 loaves so eat one and freeze one for later.

Ingredients:
3 cups flour
1 teaspoon salt
1 ½ teaspoon baking powder
3 tablespoons poppy seed
1 cup vegetable oil
3 large eggs
2 cups granulated sugar
2 teaspoons lemon juice
2 teaspoons lemon zest
1 ½ teaspoons vanilla
¼ cup lemon juice
1 teaspoon vanilla
2 cups powder sugar

Directions:

- Preheat the oven to 350 degrees F and grease two 9-inch loaf pans.

- In a large bowl combine the flour, salt, baking powder and poppy seed. Whisk to combine well.

- In a mixing bowl combine the vegetable oil and eggs. Beat until frothy.

- Add the granulated sugar and mix in well.

- Add the lemon juice, lemon zest and vanilla and mix.

- Gradually add the flour mixture to the lemon mixture until it is well combined. Make sure to scrape down the sides of the bowl as you go. You will end up with a very wet and sticky batter.

- Pour equally into the two loaf pans and bake 50 to 60 minutes or until a toothpick inserted into the center of each loaf comes out clean and the bread springs back when pressed.

- Remove the loaves to a cooling rack and let sit in the pans for about 10 minutes.

- Make the glaze by combining all ingredients in a small bowl and whisking well.

- Take s skewer and poke holes in the bread, while still in the pans. Poke several holes across and several down.

- Pour the glaze over the two loaves of poked bread in a drizzle. It will go through the holes and infuse itself into the bread.

- When the bread is nearly cool, flip it out of the loaf pan. Letting the glaze soak in and distribute through the bread for at least 3 hours makes for the best tasting bread (It tastes more like a cake).

Gourmet French Rue Omelet

Featuring: Rue

The following is an egg recipe that might not be to everyone's taste. You might find you actually like rue once you have tasted it. Rue is a little bit on the bitter side but it tastes pretty good in the following omelet. If you have problems with the blood vessels in the eye, this herb will help you strengthen them. You might as well eat a lovely omelet while do so. This makes 1 omelet.

Ingredients:
2 large eggs, beaten
1 to 2 tablespoons milk
2 teaspoons dried of fresh rue, crushed or chopped
1 tablespoon dried rosemary
1 tablespoon dried oregano
salt and pepper to taste
1 tablespoon unsalted butter

Directions:

- Break the eggs into a large bowl and whisk with the milk.

- Add the rue, rosemary, oregano, salt and pepper and whisk well.

- Heat a skillet on the stove and melt the butter.

- Pour in the egg mixture and rotate the pan carefully so the egg covers the bottom.

- Pull edges up and swirl any liquid underneath all around.

- Once the egg is firm, slide out on a plate folding the omelet onto itself to make a half circle.

- Serve immediately.

Chicken Breasts with Shallots and Spinach

Featuring: Shallot

Shallots are a mild version of the earthy onion. They are much smaller and come in clumps but are bigger than chives. I find them in the grocery with the papery wrap taken off and they are white to a light pink or lavender. They have a sweeter flavor than an onion and are considered the Cadillac of onions. The following recipe for chicken breasts with shallots and spinach makes four delicious servings.

Ingredients:

3 tablespoons unsalted butter, divided
1 tablespoon olive oil
4 skinless, boneless chicken breasts, pounded thin
salt and pepper to taste
2 shallots, peeled and chopped
1 clove garlic, peeled and minced
1/3 cup dry white wine
½ cup chicken broth
2 to 3 handfuls fresh spinach

Directions:

- Melt the 1 tablespoon of the butter in a skillet over medium heat and add the olive oil.

- Season the chicken breasts with salt and pepper on both sides and brown on both sides in the skillet over medium heat.

- Reduce heat to medium low, cover and cook about 6 to 8 minutes or until the chicken is done.

- Remove the chicken from the skillet and place on a plate. Cover with foil to keep warm.

- Place the shallots and garlic in the same skillet and sauté over medium high until tender.

- Stir in the wine and cook 5 minutes.

- Stir in the broth and cook another 5 to 7 minutes or until the liquid reduces and thickens slightly.

- Add the rest of the butter and let it melt.

- Add the fresh spinach and stir until it wilts and heats up.

- Serve the sauce over the chicken immediately.

Warm Potato Salad with Green Beans and Summer Savory

Featuring: Summer Savory

Summer savory contains thymol just like the herb thyme. It is often cooked in bean dishes to quell any buildup of gas. The following warm potato salad recipe is adapted from a recipe my grandmother used to make. It is as good in the summer as it is in the winter and best made with fresh summer savory. It makes about 6 side dishes.

Ingredients:
4 quarts of water, divided
8 ounces fresh green beans, trimmed and snapped
1 ½ pound Yukon gold potatoes, peeled and sliced
2 tablespoons shallots, minced
2 tablespoons white wine vinegar
¼ cup olive oil
2 tablespoons summer savory, chopped
Salt and pepper to taste

Directions:

- In a 4 quart or larger pot, place 2 quarts of the water over high heat and bring to a boil.

- Add the prepared green beans and boil until they turn bright green and become tender crisp, about 2 minutes. Immediately drain and rinse with cold water or drain and throw them into ice water, cool and drain.

- Place the other 2 quarts of water back in the pan over high heat and bring to a boil.

- Add the potatoes and boil until tender when poked with a fork, but not mushy, about 10 minutes. Drain and rinse with cold water to stop them from cooking. Once well drained, place in a bowl.

- In a glass measuring cup mix the shallots with the vinegar (use a glass cup to stop any chemical reactions that might not taste too good).

- In a medium saucepan over medium heat, swirl the olive oil and summer savory and sauté until the savory becomes limp and darker green. It should also be very fragrant (about 8 minutes). Do not let the oil start to sizzle.

- Pour half the oil mixture into the vinegar mixture and stir.

- Pour the other half of the oil mixture over the potatoes and toss gently.

- Top the potatoes with the green beans and drizzle the vinegar mixture over top.

- Serve immediately.

Devilled Dragon-Herb Eggs

Featuring: Tarragon

Tarragon is called the dragon herb because it resembles a dragon with curly and twisty scales. It is said to help digestive disorders so use liberally with food. Many people love deviled eggs and adding tarragon to them gives them a delightful flavor. This recipe uses 1 dozen eggs to make 24 servings.

Ingredients:
1 dozen eggs, hard boiled, cooled and peeled
1/3 cup mayonnaise
2 tablespoons prepared horseradish
1 tablespoon Dijon mustard
2 tablespoons minced garlic
2 tablespoons sweet pickle juice (no pickle)
2 teaspoons apple cider vinegar
salt and pepper to taste
4 teaspoons fresh tarragon leaves, chopped fine
2 teaspoons green onion (just the white part)
paprika

24 tarragon leaves

Directions:

- Cut the eggs lengthwise in two and carefully scoop out the yolk into a bowl and place the whites, hole up, on a plate to reserve.

- Mash the yolks well and add the mayonnaise, horseradish, mustard, garlic, pickle juice and vinegar. Mix well and season with salt and pepper.

- Add the chopped tarragon and onion and mix gently.

- Spoon the yolk filling into the indentations of the egg white. (If desired, pipe it in by placing the filling in a large plastic bag, cut off the tip in one bottom corner and squeeze it in).

- Sprinkle the tops of the eggs with a dusting of paprika and place a fresh whole leaf on top of each serving.

- Cover with plastic wrap and refrigerate at least 2 hours before serving.

English Watercress Soup

Featuring: Watercress

If you have ever been to the English countryside in the springtime, you may have encountered English watercress soup. It is a very popular dish in England with a lovely peppery flavor. It is often served with a whipped savory topping on top that will get your lips smacking for more. I put some frozen, but thawed peas in with mine after pureeing just for some texture and flavor, but they are optional.

Ingredients:
2 tablespoons vegetable oil
1 large potato, peeled and sliced
1 medium onion, peeled and chopped
¼ teaspoon salt
2 ½ cups chicken stock

2 ½ cups milk
1 ½ pound watercress, large stems removed
¼ cup heavy whipped cream
½ cup frozen, thawed peas (optional)
½ cup watercress leaves as garnish

Directions:

- In a large stock pot over high heat, add the vegetable oil. Add the potato and onion and stir to coat evenly with the oil. Season with salt and reduce heat to low simmering in the oil about 5 minutes.

- Pour in the chicken stock and milk and bring to a boil. Reduce heat and simmer 10 minutes or until the potato is tender.

- Stir in the watercress and simmer uncovered 4 to 5 minutes or until cooked.

- Blend with an immersion blender or place small batches in a blender to puree and return to the pot.

- If using the peas, add them and let them heat through.

- Whip the heavy cream in a bowl.

- Ladle the soup into 6 individual bowls, place a dollop of whipped cream on to. top with a watercress leaf and serve hot.

Pork Loin Stuffed with Cabbage, Mushrooms and Winter Savory

Featuring: Winter Savory

The peppery flavor of winter savory comes through in this stuffed pork loin that will serve four people. The loin is cut open, the filling made and spread on. The loin is then rolled like a jelly roll and cooked and then sliced making the meat look like a delightful pinwheel.

Ingredients:

2 pound pork loin
½ teaspoon salt
2 tablespoons vegetable oil
¼ cup white onion, peeled and chopped fine
2/3 cup savoy cabbage, chopped
2 cloves garlic, peeled and minced
2 tablespoons fresh flat leaf parsley, chopped fine
½ teaspoon sugar
2 tablespoons dried porcini mushrooms, chopped
¼ teaspoon salt
¼ teaspoon pepper
¼ cup olive oil

Directions:

- Preheat the oven to 425 degrees F.

- Salt all sides of the pork loin and set it on a cutting board. Using a sharp knife, cut 2/3 from the top (height) down along the entire side from end to end. Do not cut through to make 2 pieces. Just open it up and lay the loin flat.

- Place the onion, cabbage, garlic, parsley, sugar, porcinis, salt, pepper and olive oil in a food processor and pulse until it looks a little chunky, like rough pesto. It should be spreadable.

- Spread the filling evenly on the pork loin and roll jelly roll style. Tie it with baking twine.

- Place an ovenproof skillet over medium high heat and add the 2 tablespoons of vegetable oil. Brown the pork loin on all sides. Place the skillet in the oven for 20 to 25 minutes. (If you do not have an ovenproof skillet, place in a baking pan sprayed with non-stick spray).

- Check the internal temperature with an instant thermometer. It should read 155 degrees F. The actual temperature of pork should be 160 degrees F, but as the roast rests, the temperature should go up to 160. Let the roast rest in the pan 5 to 10 minutes. Remove to a cutting board, cut of the twin and slice into rounds.

Chapter 3 is all about herbs that lend dimension to a dish. The flavors can be mild or strong and there is usually nothing else that tastes just like them. They would be very much missed if they were not added to give the food extra dimension, texture, scent and taste.

Chapter 3: Unique and Bold Herbs and Spices

I cannot imagine chicken salad without the bright flavor of celery seed or Middle Eastern tabouli without the fresh flavor of mint. The herbs featured in this chapter are those that are definitely missed if they aren't there. They are herbs and spices with strong flavors or give it texture or give it color. Some of these herbs and spices may never have crossed your kitchen cupboards, like Nigella Seed or Bayberry and I am hoping I am bringing some new flavors to your food. These herbs come from all over the world and some are familiar while others are not.

Wild Game Pot Roast with Bayberries

Featuring: Bayberry

The following recipe is good for a venison roast, but you can alter it and use it for wild turkey or wild boar as well. The ingredients are made into a lovely marinade and it is important for it to be placed in a glass container (no metal) because it will react and make things taste strange. I suggest marinating boar or venison 2 to 3 days and turkey 1 to 2 days. Gingersnaps used in this dish are the kind you buy in the box at the grocery. Dried bayberries are usually found in specialty herb and spice stores and they are a little bit expensive. The fresh ones are really hard to find unless you have a bayberry bush and save them. The berries are really beautiful white with black specks and they look a little waxy. The flavor is very unique.

Ingredients:
2 cups water
1 cup apple cider vinegar
3 cups onion (large onion), peeled and sliced, divided
10 whole cloves
4 fresh bayberry leaves or 2 dried ones
2 tablespoons brown sugar
1 tablespoon juniper berries
1 teaspoon peppercorns

1 4 pound deer hind quarter roast
1 cup celery, chopped
2 cups carrot, peeled and chopped
10 small gingersnaps, crushed

Directions:

- Combine the ingredients for the marinade in a saucepan including the water, vinegar, 1 cup of the onion (reserve the rest), cloves, brown sugar, juniper berries and peppercorns. Bring to a boil and immediately bring to a simmer for about 5 minutes or until the sugar dissolves.

- Place the meat in a big glass dish. Pour the hot marinade over top and cover. Let cool and place in the refrigerator 2 to 3 days.

- Remove from refrigerator, remove the meat from the marinade and pat dry. Braise on both sides. Reserve the marinade and place meat in a Dutch Oven.

- Add the rest of the onion, celery and carrots in the Dutch Oven with the meat.

- Add half the marinade saving the rest for later.

- Bring to a boil and simmer on low for about 5 hours or until the meat falls apart.

- Add the remaining marinade as needed so the pot does not dry out.

- Remove the meat to a platter.

- Add the crushed gingersnaps to the liquid in the Dutch Oven and heat until it thickens. Serve over the meat.

Banana, Strawberry with Aloe Smoothie

Featuring: Aloe Vera

Aloe gel is very nutritious and healing. Just cut a leaf longways to remove the skin from both sides and you will see that the gel stays together like a thicker version of gelatin. It does have some flavor but it also makes the smoothie below thicker. I have a very large aloe Vera plant in my kitchen bay window but you can also purchase whole leaves at many grocery stores. This smoothie is delicious and filled with all kinds of vitamins. I like to drink it in the morning to give me a good start to the day.

Ingredients:
1 banana, peeled
1 ½ cups almond milk, unsweetened
4 large strawberries, hulled and quartered
1 cup fresh aloe Vera gel cubes, as above
½ cup ice

Directions:

- Place all items in a blender and blend until smooth.

- Pour into a large glass and drink immediately.

Gluten Free and Safe Arrowroot Pancakes

Featuring: Arrowroot

Arrowroot is what teething cookies are made of, so if it is safe for baby – it is safe for those that might have problems with flour. The following pancakes are very tasty and safe for most people to eat. I make them for a friend that has a gluten sensitivity and they do not bother her at all.

Ingredients:

2 tablespoon coconut oil
1 cup almond milk, unsweetened
1 teaspoon apple cider vinegar
5 eggs, beaten
¼ cup almond flour, packed
½ cup coconut flour
½ cup arrowroot

2 tablespoons honey

Directions:

- Melt coconut oil in a large skillet over medium heat.

- Place the almond milk, vinegar, eggs, almond flour, coconut flour, arrowroot and honey in a blender and blend until it is smooth.

- Use a big spoon to pour in the skillet to make pancakes and smooth with the back of the spoon. I do 3 at a time.

- Cook each side until the pancake rises and browns.

- Serve drizzled with more honey and some fruit or jam if desired.

Spicy and Luscious Calendula Paella

Featuring: Calendula

Paella is made with either fish or chicken, vegetables, rice and some spicy seasoning. The seasoning usually makes the rice yellow to orange and it tastes delectable. Calendula gives the same color as the more expensive saffron, and the flavor is different being peppery and very tangy. It gives just the right amount of zing to culinary dishes. The following paella recipe has many ingredients and takes time to make, but you will want to make it over and over. It is definitely a showstopper. It makes enough for 6 to 8 servings too and the color is just lovely.

Ingredients:
4 cups chicken broth
2 ½ cups uncooked long grain rice
1 cup onion, peeled and chopped
4 cloves garlic, peeled and chopped, divided
1/2 teaspoon salt
½ teaspoon turmeric
¼ teaspoon pepper
1 bay leaf

1 large green or red bell pepper, seeded and julienned
3 green onions, sliced
1 teaspoon fresh parsley, minced
1 teaspoon dry thyme
¼ - ½ teaspoon hot sauce (depends on how hot you want it)
2 tablespoons olive oil
1 cup mushrooms, cleaned and sliced
2 medium tomatoes, chopped
1 10 ounce package frozen peas
½ pound fresh or frozen uncooked shrimp, peeled and deveined
1 pound boneless, skinless chicken breast, sliced thin
2 tablespoons lemon juice
½ cup fresh calendula petals (about 12 blossoms)

Directions:

- In a saucepan combine the broth, rice, onion, half of the garlic, salt, turmeric, pepper and the bay leaf. Bring the mixture to a boil and reduce. Cover and simmer 20 minutes or until the rice is tender.

- In a Dutch Oven sauté the bell pepper, green onion, parsley, thyme, hot sauce, the remaining garlic and in the olive oil for about 2 minutes.

- Add in the mushrooms and sauté until the bell peppers are tender-crisp.

- Add the tomato and then the frozen peas (they should still be frozen because it adds moisture) and heat through.

- Remove the bay leaf from the rice mixture and pour the rice mixture in the Dutch oven. Keep this warm and stirring to prevent from burning.

- Take a skillet and add the shrimp and lemon juice and cook over medium high heat for about 2 minutes. Add the chicken and cook until the it is no longer pink, about 3 to 5 minutes, stirring constantly.

- Add the shrimp/chicken mixture to the Dutch Oven and combine well.

- Sprinkle the calendula petals over top, mix and serve.

Fresh Chicken Salad with Refreshing Celery Seed

Featuring: Celery Seed

Celery seed has a bright flavor that is welcome in all kinds of dishes. Try it in soups and stews or with chicken. The seed lasts for a long time in an airtight container, about 3 years, which will allow you to make a lot of chicken salad with the following recipe.

Ingredients:
2 boneless, skinless chicken breast halves, cooked and shredded
½ cup mayonnaise
½ teaspoon Dijon or Honey Mustard
¼ teaspoon celery seed
2 tablespoons celery leaves, chopped
¼ teaspoon ground black pepper
Optional: Add ¼ cup chopped celery

Directions:
- Shred or chop the chicken in small pieces after it cools.

- In a bowl, combine the mayonnaise, mustard, celery seed, celery leaves and pepper (also the celery if using) and mix well.

- Add the chicken and fold in.

- Cover and refrigerate 30 minutes to overnight. Let warm a bit before serving in lettuce cups or on bread.

Sautéed Bitter Yet Delicious Chicory Leaves

Featuring: Chicory

If you live in the Mid-West or Northern Eastern states you have probably seen chicory growing on the side of the road. The beautiful raggedy blue flowers on stiff stalks is a regular growing wild. Many people add it to coffee to mellow it out but my favorite way to eat chicory is like a vegetable. It tastes much like spinach but chewy. I will sometimes add a teaspoon of vinegar to the mix to just to give it a more acid presence. Do not eat the plants that grow on the side of the road because they are most likely contaminated with toxins from traffic. I grow a patch of chicory in my backyard and sometimes I do find it in the grocery store.

Ingredients:
1 pound chicory stems and leaves
2 to 3 tablespoons olive oil
2 cloves garlic, peeled and chopped
½ teaspoon salt
1 pinch red pepper flakes, crushed
lemon juice or vinegar

Directions:

* Wash the leaves well and drain at least 3 times. The leaves are hairy and hold on to debris so washing more than once is essential to get any dirt or dust out of them.

* Boil in water that does not have salt in it. Test to see when the stems are tender and drain.

* Let cool and dry off with a paper towel.

* Heat a medium sized frying pan and add the olive oil. Throw in the garlic and sauté for a few minutes.

* Add the chicory, salt and pepper flakes and sauté about 2 minutes.

* Turn off the stove and add the juice of a lemon or vinegar (try both if you like) and serve immediately.

Irish Potato Casserole with Cream Cheese and Chives

Featuring: Chives

I have had a chive plant for over 10 years. It grows in a big pot and I put the pot in my breezeway during the winter. The first sign of spring the pot starts to sprout. The following recipe is a good way to use chives and it makes 8 side dishes and it is good enough to serve as a main dish too. Instead of the russet potatoes, I will use 10 to 12 smaller red potatoes and I do not remove the skin from them.

Ingredients:
8 medium russet potatoes, peeled and cubed
1 8 ounce package cream cheese, room temperature
1 8 ounce container sour cream
½ cup butter, softened
½ teaspoon salt
¼ teaspoon pepper
¼ cup fresh chives, minced
1 shake paprika

Directions:

- Boil the potatoes in water and then bring to a simmer for about 20 minutes or until they are tender but not falling apart.

- Drain the potatoes, but do not rinse with cold water.

- Place potatoes in a large bowl and set aside.

- In another bowl, combine the cream cheese, sour cream and butter and mash until it is creamy. Add the salt and pepper and mix in.

- Fold the cream cheese mixture into the potatoes and mix well.

- Pour into a greased 2 quart casserole, sprinkle with chives and paprika.

- Cook in a preheated 350 degree F oven for about 30 minutes. If they get too brown, cover with foil.

- Let sit about 5 minutes and spoon out of the pan and onto a plate.

Middle Eastern Minty Tabouli

Featuring: Mint

Tabouli is a Middle Eastern salad made with bulgur wheat. It is very nutritious and full of fiber and minty flavor. Mint is used in a variety of dishes and should never be relegated to iced tea. This recipe makes 6 servings.

Ingredients:
½ cup extra-fine bulgur wheat
4 firm Roma tomatoes, finely chopped
1 English cucumber (no seeds), skin on, finely chopped
2 bunches fresh parsley, stems removed and finely chopped
12 to 15 fresh mint leaves, finely chopped
4 green onions, green and white part finely chopped
Salt to taste
3 to 4 tablespoons fresh lime juice
3 to 4 tablespoons extra virgin olive oil
Romaine lettuce leaves

Directions:

- Wash the bulgur wheat two times and then soak in warm water (not hot) to cover 5 to 7 minutes or until it softens. Drain and squeeze by hand. I use a screen sieve and press down on it to get all the water out. Place in a clean paper towel and squeeze again. Place the bulgur into a bowl and set aside.

- Chop the tomatoes and squeeze in the sieve and paper towels to remove the liquid. Place in a serving bowl.

- Chop the cucumber, parsley, mint and green onions and add to the bowl with the tomatoes.

- Add the bulgur and the salt and mix well.

- In a small bowl combine the lime juice and olive oil and whisk well. Pour over the bulgur and combine.

- Cover with plastic wrap and refrigerate at least 3 hours or overnight.

- Place a leaf of lettuce on a plate and spoon the tabouli in to serve.

Tangy Mustard Encrusted Pork Chops

Featuring: Mustard

The following recipe is for tangy flavored pork chops that will wake up the taste buds and make them very happy. Not only does the mustard make it flavorful, but the chops are also served with some peach jam, which sounds a little strange, but it is delicious. It makes 8 servings and it is most flavorful when you marinate the chops overnight or at least 3 hours.

Ingredients:
8 bone-in, 1-inch thick pork chops
2 tablespoons ground mustard
2 tablespoons garlic powder
1 tablespoon smoked paprika
1 ½ teaspoons ground black pepper
½ teaspoon kosher salt, or to taste
1/3 cup olive oil
Peach jam

Directions:

- Prepare a 9 x 13-inch baking pan with non-stick spray and place the chops in it.

- In a small bowl, mix the mustard, garlic powder, paprika, pepper and salt and whisk to combine well.

- Rub this mixture over the pork chops, front and back. and place back into the baking pan.

- Cover the baking pan with plastic wrap and let sit at least 1 hour at room temperature. Place the chops in the refrigerator overnight or at least 3 hours.

- Heat the oil in a skillet, a cast iron one works best, over medium high heat. Place some of the chops in the skillet, brown, flip once and brown the other side (about 10 minutes). Do this in batches. The chops should be cooked through.

- Serve with some peach jam.

Cauliflower - Nigella Seed Side Dish

Featuring: Nigella Seed

I will bet not many readers have ever heard of nigella seed and didn't know you could cook with it. It has a strange flavor of a little bit of onion, a little bit a sesame seed and a little bit of poppy seed and the whole or crushed seeds give a dish some crunch. I particularly enjoy eating it by sprinkling it on top of vegetables. Nigella seed is very healing and was used to heal just about everything in the past. The following recipe makes for a great side dish and makes 4 servings. Anyone who likes cauliflower will love this dish.

Ingredients:
½ small cauliflower, cut in florets
2 teaspoons vegetable oil
1 teaspoon nigella seed
1 teaspoon red chili powder
2 tablespoons water
salt to taste

Directions:

- Steam the cauliflower florets for 6 to 7 minutes until soft but not mushy.

- Heat the oil in a skillet and add the nigella seed. Sauté 1 minute until they let go of their fragrance.

- Add the cauliflower and stir turning to low.

- In a small bowl, mix the chili powder with the water and immediately pour into the cauliflower. Sauté 4 minutes or until the water evaporates.

- Season with salt and serve.

Delicate Salad Burnet Cream Cheese Tea Sandwich Filling

Featuring: Salad Burnet

I enjoy attending formal teas and this recipe is one that is perfect for that type of event, although I have been known to slap some of this filling between two slices of bread and take them to work. I take white, wheat or rye bread, cut off the crusts and use the spread inside with a leaf of lettuce. I then cut the sandwiches into little squares or shapes with cookie cutters to serve with tea.

Ingredients:
16 ounces cream cheese, at room temperature
½ cup butter, at room temperature
¼ cup milk or light cream
2 tablespoons chives, chopped
¼ cup salad burnet, chopped

Directions:

- In a bowl, combine the cream cheese and butter and use a fork to mash all together.

- Add the milk or cream and use a wire whip to get the mixture as smooth as possible. It will be thick.

- Sprinkle in the chives and salad burnet and mix well.

- Spread on one piece of bread and top with a lettuce leaf and another piece of bread.

Sweet and Tart Rhubarb and Sweet Cicely Compote

Featuring: Sweet Cicely

I enjoy the flavor and texture of cooked rhubarb, but no one else in my house does. I make a rhubarb compote that I mix in yogurt or with equal parts whipped cream for a lovely dessert. I can freeze this compote and use as much as I like, when I want it. I have also put it in a baked pie crust, put it in the refrigerator for a few hours and served with whipped cream. There is no sugar in the recipe and amazingly the compote is sweet because of the sweet cicely, but if you feel you need more sugar, add a few teaspoons into the mix along with the honey.

Ingredients:
2 cups rhubarb, chopped
1 inch piece of fresh ginger, peeled and grated
1 cup sweet cicely leaves and stems, chopped
2 tablespoons honey

Directions:

- In a saucepan, combine the rhubarb, ginger, sweet cicely and honey and heat over medium heat. The rhubarb should release liquid and should come to a boil.

- Once it boils, reduce to a simmer and simmer about 10 minutes. If it looks like it is drying out, add up to 1 tablespoon water.

- Rhubarb should be soft when it is done. Remove from heat and cool in the pan.

- Once cool, place in a covered dish and use as will.

May Day May Wine

Featuring: Sweet Woodruff

May day has always been an important day for my family. It is the opening day of spring and since we all love to garden; it is the start of our favorite season. I love May wine and would feel sad if I couldn't have a bit every May Day. It is traditionally made with white wine and I usually use a Riesling. I have made it non-alcoholic with sparkling white grape juice too and it was very good. Place your May wine in a big punch bowl and float some strawberries and sweet woodruff leaves on top. I airdry some sweet woodruff just for this every fall. The recipe calls for dried and fresh woodruff and there is good reason. The dried has more flavor and the infusion is much stronger than using fresh. You might have to wait a year before making this treat. If you want to make the non-alcoholic substitute use a non-alcoholic white grape juice for the Riesling and sparkling apple cider for the Champaign.

Ingredients:
½ cup dried sweet woodruff leaves,
1 bottle Riesling wine
1 bottle chilled German Sekt or Champaign (I like Champaign better)
1 cup fresh strawberries, chopped and divided + a handful of whole strawberries
A handful of fresh sweet woodruff leaves and flowers

Directions:

- Infuse the dried sweet woodruff leaves and ¼ cup of the chopped strawberries in the Riesling for about 3 hours or overnight. (Overnight is a little long and the flavor is a little too strong for me)

- Strain the Riesling into a punch bowl and discard the infused leaves and strawberries.

- Pour in the Champaign, watch it doesn't bubble over.

- Pour in the remaining chopped strawberries and place the whole ones in a bowl.

- Sprinkle the fresh woodruff leaves and flowers on top and stir carefully.

- Ladle out into glasses and place a whole strawberry in each glass.

Light and Fluffy Vanilla Scones

Featuring: Vanilla

The following recipe makes the most delicious vanilla flavored scones and it is made with both vanilla extract and vanilla beans. Taking vanilla directly from the bean ensures a delicious vanilla flavor. Since the beans are very expensive, I do sometimes used pure vanilla extract, but try to stay away from imitation vanilla. The flavor is just not the same. These scones are light fluffy and flavorful and the recipe makes 16 scones.

Ingredients:
2 cups flour
2 teaspoons baking powder
6 tablespoons granulated sugar
½ teaspoon kosher salt
½ cup cold butter cut in ½-inch cubes
1 egg, slightly beaten
½ cup + 1 Tbsp heavy whipping cream
1 vanilla bean, seeds scooped out
1 teaspoon vanilla extract
Another egg, slightly beaten
2 tablespoons coarse sugar

Directions:

- Preheat the oven to 375 degrees F.

- In a food processor, layer the flour, baking powder, sugar and salt.

- Pulse to mix.

- Add the butter cubes and pulse 10 times. The mixture should resemble a coarse meal.

- In a bowl, whisk the egg with the cream and add the vanilla bean seeds and extract. Whisk in well.

- Gradually add the dry ingredients to the wet using a whisk at first and then a wooden spoon.

- Turn dough out on a floured surface and form into a ball. Divide the ball in half and make 2 rounds that are somewhat flat, about 6 to 7-inches in diameter and 3/4-inch thick.

- Cut each round into 8 wedges and place the wedges on a parchment paper covered baking sheet.

- Brush each wedge with egg and sprinkle with coarse sugar.

- Bake 17 minutes or until golden brown.

- Let cool before serving.

Chapter 4 is an ethnic sort of chapter with recipes from all over
    the world and using
interesting and exotic herbs and spices that you might just have to
    send away over the
Internet to get.

Chapter 4: Exotic Herbs and Spices

Make dishes from exotic places like India, the Middle East, Mexico, Puerto Rica, the Tropics, Germany and many more with exotic herbs and spices. Today we are very lucky because we can transport foods from other lands easier than we could just a few years ago. I nerve heard of Ajwan or Galangal until just a few years ago. You may have a hard time growing these herbs and spices because most of them take special conditions. You will have to rely on buying them at specialty or grocery stores that have a wide variety of world products.

Deep Fried Spicy Ajwan Bread

Featuring: Ajwan

The following recipe is a deep fried flat bread common in India using ingredients commonly found in the grocery store. I am sure it tastes much different in India, but this version is very good and I love to serve it with dinner or lunch with a salad. The Ajwan makes the flavor of the bread very memorable.

Ingredients:
2 cups all-purpose flour
2 teaspoon Ajwan seed, crushed slightly with mortar and pestle
½ teaspoon salt
1 teaspoon vegetable oil
water
vegetable oil for frying

Directions:

- In a bowl, combine the flour, crushed Ajwan seed and salt. Whisk well to combine.

- Add 1 teaspoon of the vegetable oil and mix with a wooden spoon.

- Add enough water to make a firm dough that is still a little sticky but does not stick all the way to the hands.

- Knead the bread on a flat surface, but do not knead or put hands in more flour.

- Roll the dough out between two pieces of wax paper very thin.

- Cut the dough using a 1 ½-inch circle cooking cutter.

- Prick each circle several times with a fork.

- Heat oil and drop circles in hot oil to fry over medium heat until they are slightly puffy and golden brown on both sides.

- Drain on plates covered with paper towels and cool.

- Store in airtight containers. This makes 80 circles and they last 2 to 3 days.

Spiced Chickpea Curry with Mango Flavored Amchur Powder

Featuring: Amchur powder

Amchur powder is made from dried crushed mangos and is very fruity and delicious. It is good for removing toxins from the body in a very luscious manner. This recipe is a nice Indian style recipe using chickpeas to make a curry. It serves 4 and is very spicy and also a vegetarian dish.

Ingredients:
2 tablespoons vegetable oil
2 cinnamon sticks
1 teaspoon cumin seeds
3 cardamom pods (black or green)
2 tomatoes, diced
2 ½ tablespoons amchur powder
1 teaspoon sea salt
3 teaspoons coriander seeds
1 teaspoon Garam Marsala
½ teaspoon cayenne
½ teaspoon turmeric

1 teaspoon light brown sugar
¼ cup fresh cilantro, chopped and divided
1 15 ounce can chickpeas, washed and drained
1 cup water
¼ cup onion, peeled and chopped fine
plain yogurt for topping

Directions:

- Heat the oil in a Dutch oven over medium high heat. Add the cinnamon sticks, cumin seeds and cardamom pods and stir cooking for a few seconds until it gets fragrant.

- Stir in the tomatoes, amchur powder, salt, coriander seeds, Garam marsala, cayenne, turmeric and brown sugar. Turn the heat to medium low and simmer 10 minutes with the lid partially on.

- Stir in half of the cilantro and save the rest for garnish. Add the chickpeas and the water, stir, cover and simmer for 20 minutes or until the sauce thickens, stirring occasionally.

- Serve over rice with onions, cilantro and yogurt for garnish.

Indian Pomegranate Flavored Aloo Anardana

Featuring: Anardana

I love anardana with potatoes and the following is a Middle Eastern recipe using them to make a delicious dish that will feed 4 to 6 as a main or side dish. Potatoes in that area are not like russet potatoes that we have here in America. I prefer red skin potatoes but have used Yukon Gold too. Do not peel the potatoes if using red ones because the peels are good for you and give the dish more substance. This recipe calls for ghee, which is a fat used in Middle Eastern Dishes. I found jars of ghee in a discount grocery store the other day and you can find it in Middle Eastern stores. It also requires finely powdered anardana and if yours seems a little coarse, just put it through a spice chopper or in the blender and make it a little finer.

Ingredients:
1 ½ pounds red potatoes, cut in about 1 inch cubes (not peeled)
2 cups ghee
3 whole red chilies
¾ teaspoon cumin powder
½ tablespoon coriander powder
½ teaspoon chili powder
¼ teaspoon Turmeric
1 teaspoon sea salt
½ cup Anardana, finely powdered

Directions:

- Boil the potatoes in a pot of water until they are tender, but the skins are not totally falling off. Drain and let cool to room temperature.

- In a large wok or Dutch oven, heat the ghee until it melts.

- Add the whole red chilis and fry in the ghee until they change color (only a few seconds).

- Add the chopped potatoes and stir fry until the potatoes turn pink and crispy.

- While potatoes are frying, mix the cumin, coriander, chili powder, turmeric and sea salt in a small bowl.

- Sprinkle the spices over the potatoes and stir to make sure all the potatoes are coated.

- Add the Anardana and mix well. Fry four a few more minutes and serve hot.

Surprisingly Savory Asafoetida Mushrooms

Featuring: Asafoetida

Warning – Asafoetida stinks until you start cooking with it. Don't let that turn you off from using it because it will surprise you with the big punch of savory flavor. The following mushroom side dish is hot and spicy yet very savory due to the inclusion of Asafoetida. Mushrooms soak up anything you cook them in and take on that flavor, so they are a perfect paring with Asafoetida. It makes 2 to 3 side servings that go well with just about any meat or vegetable.

Ingredients:

2 tablespoons vegetable oil
1 generous pinch of Asafoetida
1 ½ pound mushrooms, trimmed – stemmed and quartered
2 small dried red chili peppers, chopped
½ teaspoon turmeric
1 cup crushed tomatoes
salt and pepper to taste

Directions:

- When the spice darkens (just a few seconds), add the mushrooms, chili pepper, turmeric, tomatoes and salt and pepper and stir to combine.

- Cover, lower the heat to a simmer and let go about 15 to 20 minutes or until the liquid absorbs. Keep an eye on it after about 10 minutes so it does not completely evaporate and burn.

- Serve hot.

Classic Mexican Bean Recipe Featuring Epazote

Featuring: Epazote

The recipe I chose for Epazote is a bean dish, a popular dish for using epazote. Good thing too, because epazote helps to cut down on gas, which beans produce. There are other strong flavors that mask the huge flavor of the herb and help it to combine better. This is an authentic Mexican recipe and I use dried black beans and a ceramic bean pot given to me by a friend from Mexico. You can use a Dutch oven if you cannot find a bean pot that goes over a gas burner. This recipe will serve 4 to 6 people.

Ingredients:

2 cups dried black beans
½ cup white onion, peeled and cut in large chunks
2 cloves garlic, peeled and crushed with hand
water
2 to 3 leaves fresh epazote leaves, whole
salt to taste
1 whole Serrano or Jalapeno chili, top cut off and seeded but still whole
Flour tortillas
Toppings: Shredded cheese, salsa, chopped green onion, chopped cilantro

Directions:

- Sort the beans and soak in enough water to cover with lid on, in the refrigerator overnight.

- Drain the beans and rinse two times.

- Place the beans in a lidded ceramic pot (bean pot).

- Add the onion, garlic and enough water to come 3 inches over the bean mixture. Bring to a boil.

- Remove any floating beans and scrape the foam.

- Reduce to a simmer and stir occasionally. Make sure water is always at least 1-inch above the beans.

- After 1 hour, add the epazote and simmer covered, stirring occasionally, until the beans are soft (about 1 ½ to 3 hours).

- Season with salt and add the Serrano or Jalapeno peppers and let simmer another 10 minutes.

- Remove the pieces of onion, garlic, peppers and epazote leaves.

- Use a fork to mash some of the beans against the side of the pot and let the mixture thicken while simmering a little longer.

- Serve on tortillas with toppings.

Tangy Chicken Curry with Fenugreek

Featuring: Fenugreek

Fenugreek is especially good for digestive issues making it perfect for many recipes and cooking in general. The following is a curry recipe that is very good and uses fenugreek leaves. It makes 6 to 8 servings and is very spicy. The interesting part of this recipe is that you grind your onions into a paste and use it. The dish is extremely flavorful.

Ingredients:

2 4 tablespoons vegetable oil, divided
2 large onions, peeled and sliced thin
2 large tomatoes, diced
2 tablespoons garlic powder
1 tablespoon ginger paste
2 teaspoons coriander powder
1 teaspoon cumin
½ teaspoon red chili powder
½ teaspoon turmeric
2 teaspoons Garam Marsala
pounds chicken, cut in bite size pieces (use any parts you want)
Salt to taste
1 pound fresh fenugreek leaves, chopped
½ cup or more hot water

Directions:

- Heat the 2 tablespoons of the oil over medium heat in a Dutch oven.

- Sauté the onion until it is golden brown.

- Remove onions and place on paper towel over a plate. Turn off the heat.

- Grind the onions to a smooth past in a food processor (do not use any water).

- Place the onion paste in a small bowl.

- In the food processor, place the tomatoes, garlic, ginger paste and pulse until smooth and scrap into another small bowl or container.

- Heat the other 2 tablespoons oil in the Dutch oven. Add onion paste and sauté 2 minutes.

- Add the tomato mixture and garlic, ginger, coriander, cumin, red chili powder, turmeric and Garam Marsala and mix. Sauté on low about 10 minutes or until the oil starts to separate.

- Season the chicken pieces with salt and pepper and add to the pan. Sauté until the chicken is browned.

- Add the fenugreek leaves and stir in.

- Add hot water, stir and cover the pot. Simmer until the chicken is done and if the pan starts to dry out add a little more hot water. Stir occasionally to keep from burning. The mixture will thicken as it cooks.

- Serve with flat bread, Naan or rice.

Fit for A King Thai Coconut Galangal Soup

Featuring: Galangal

I found galangal when a friend visited from Thailand. She wanted to make an authentic Thai soup called Tom Yum Un and needed the spice to make it taste right. This spice rids the body of toxins and is an anti-inflammatory so no wonder my friend from Thailand was so healthy. The recipe below is taken from Tom Yum Un soup and serves 8 bowls full of creamy and spicy deliciousness.

Ingredients:
2 cups light coconut milk
7 thin slices of peeled galangal root
3 stalks lemongrass, cut in 1-inch long pieces and pounded to bruise
1 medium sweet potato, peeled cut in 1-inch rounds

4 kaffir lime leaves, torn
5 cups water
1 tablespoon pink salt
2 ½ teaspoons fresh squeezed lime juice
1 bunch fresh cilantro to use for garnish

Directions:

- Place the coconut milk in a large pot over medium high heat and bring it to a boil.

- Add the galangal slices, lemongrass, sweet potato and kaffir lime leaves and lower the heat to medium low.

- Add the water and turn to a simmer for about 45 minutes to 1 hour.

- Turn off the heat and let stand 20 minutes covered. This will allow the soup to marinate.

- Remove the galangal slices, lemongrass, sweet potato and kaffir lime leaves and discard them.

- Season with the pink salt and lime juice and garnish with cilantro.

NOTE: If it has cooled too much, warm it up to steaming hot again before serving.

German Lentil Soup

Featuring: Hamburg Parsley

Hamburg Parsley is much different that Italian flat leaf or curly parsley, in fact, it does not use leaves but the white carrot-like root. In Germany, they make a lovely lentil soup that is flavored with Hamburg parsley. The following recipe makes 4 to 6 servings and it is very hardy and delicious.

Ingredients:
2 tablespoons olive oil
2 onions, peeled and chopped

2 carrots, peeled and chopped
1 rib celery chopped
1 large parsley root, chopped
1 pound dried lentils, washed and drained several times
2 whole black pepper corns, whole
2 whole cloves
2 bay leaves
4 cups vegetable or chicken stock
1 large potato, peeled and grated
salt and pepper to taste
2 tablespoons vinegar

Directions:

- Heat the oil in a large soup pot and add the onion, carrots, celery and parsley root. Sauté to a golden brown.

- Add the lentils, pepper corns, cloves, bay leaves and the stock.

- Add the grated potato and bring to a boil.

- Reduce heat to a simmer and cover the pot simmering for 1 hour or until the lentils become tender.

- Remove the bay leaves, cloves and pepper corns.

- Add the salt and pepper.

- Add the vinegar right before serving.

Traditional Armenian Easter Bread

Featuring: Mahleb

It is very hard to find Mahleb unless you have a specialty herb and spice store around. We Americans are missing out on a very lovely flavor because of that. Along with being a good thing to clear up the congestion of a cold, it also cures digestive problems. The following recipe is for Armenian Easter Bread and it is nothing like other vanilla or anise flavored Easter Breads. It actually tastes like almond flavored cherry bread. This recipe makes 1 loaf.

Ingredients:

1 cup whole milk
2 cups unsalted butter, at room temperature
1 cup sugar
½ cup lukewarm water
2 teaspoons more sugar
2 1/4-ounce envelope active dry yeast
5 eggs
6 cups flour (more or less)
1 ½ teaspoon ground mahleb
1 ½ teaspoon baking powder
½ teaspoon salt
another egg, beaten
1 tablespoon sesame seeds

Directions:

- In a saucepan over medium heat, place the milk and butter heat until the butter melts but do not let it boil.

- Stir in the 1 cup of sugar until it dissolves. Set aside to cool to lukewarm.

- In a bowl, dissolve the 2 teaspoons sugar in the lukewarm water. Sprinkle the yeast in and let stand until it is frothy, about 10 minutes.

- In another large bowl, beat the eggs and pour some of the heated milk mixture in while whisking so the eggs do not curdle. Keep adding until it is all combined and cool a little longer.

- Add the yeast and stir until combined.

- In another large bowl, whisk the flour, mahleb, baking powder and salt with a whisk. Make a well in the middle and pour in the wet ingredients.

- Stir with a fork, little by little incorporating the wet with the dry ingredients to make a sticky dough.

- Remove dough to a flowered surface and knead for 10 minutes. Place in an oiled bowl and let rise 2 hours until it is double.

- Punch down and let double again for about 1 hour.

- Cut the dough in 5 even portions and cut in 3 equal sections. Roll to make ropes about 12 inches long and braid them together pinching the ends to seal.

- Place on parchment covered baking sheets about 4-inches apart and let rise. When the dough stays indented when poked with a finger, it is ready to bake.

- Preheat the oven to 350 degrees.

- Brush each braid with the 1 egg, beaten and sprinkle with sesame seeds.

- Bake 25 minutes, remove from the oven and cool on racks.

Exotic Banana Pineapple Sage Smoothie

Featuring: Pineapple Sage

Pineapple sage is a beautiful plant with bright green leaves and scarlet flowers. It helps with digestive complaints and calms the nerves. Try this smoothie on a hot summer morning and I guarantee you will be happy and healthy the rest of the day. The recipe asks for vanilla flavored yogurt, but I have used blueberry or banana and even lemon yogurt and the pineapple flavor will still shine through. If you use pineapple yogurt, it is a little too much.

Ingredients:
1 small banana, peeled and cut in chunks
¾ cup vanilla flavored yogurt
1 teaspoon honey
1/3 cup skim milk
3 to 4 pineapple sage leaves, chopped
½ teaspoon cinnamon (optional but it does lend a nice flavor)

Directions:

- Place the banana chunks in a blender and pulse to break them up a few times.

- Add the yogurt, honey, milk and pineapple sage leaves and blend until thick and smooth.

- Pour into two small glasses or one large one and sprinkle with the cinnamon on top.

- With a butter knife, insert the tip into the smoothie surface and swirl the cinnamon to mix in and make a design on the smoothie.

Pretty Pink Rose Petal Bread

Featuring: Rose Petals

The following recipe was given to me by a chef at a Renaissance Faire and it is deliciously crusty. The secret is to place a small quantity of water in a pan at the bottom rack of the oven and then also spraying the dough with a light mist of water before baking. Do not skip this step if you want a crusty bread. This makes 1 flavorful loaf of bread and rose petals never tasted so good.

Ingredients:
¼ cup wheat flour
3 1/3 cups bread flour (do not use all-purpose)
1 ½ teaspoon fine sea salt
1 ¼ teaspoon dry yeast
1 cup water
1/3 cup rose water
1 teaspoon honey
¼ cup rose petals, chopped
vegetable oil
cornmeal

Directions:

- In a medium sized bowl, combine the wheat flour, bread flour, salt and dry yeast and whisk to combine.

- In another bowl, combine the water with the rose water.

- Add the honey to the water mixture and whisk in well.

- Make a well in the center of the flour mixture and pour in the water mixture. Using a fork, gradually mix in all together until a sticky dough is created. Use a wooden spoon and elbow grease at the end.

- Form the dough into a ball and place on a floured board. Knead to make sure everything is combined and start adding rose petals while kneading until the dough is smooth and elastic, but still sticky. Use all the petals.

- Coat a bowl with vegetable oil and put the dough in turning to coat both sides. Cover with plastic wrap and let rise 1 hour or until doubled.

- Line a cookie sheet with parchment paper and sprinkle it with cornmeal.

- Punch down the dough to deflate. Shape into a ball and flatten placing it on the cooking sheet. Cover with oiled plastic wrap and let rise 45 minutes.

- Preheat the oven to 450 degrees F. Cut an "X" in the top of the dough and spray the top with cool water.

- Place the dough on the top shelf of the oven and place a shallow pan of water on the bottom rack.

- Bake 10 minutes and reduce the heat to 425 degrees F. Cook for 15 to 20 minutes until golden brown, firm and a toothpick inserted into the center comes out clean.

- Cool completely on a rack before cutting and serving.

Elegant Saffron Lemon Chicken

Featuring: Saffron

No doubt, saffron is the most expensive herb out there. Just a few threads cost 10 to 20 dollars. The spice is from a special orchid and comes from the anthers of the flower. Saffron does look like thin golden or orange threads and it is usually sold in plastic or glass tubes. A little goes a long way and that is fortunate because it does not keep long. The following chicken recipe makes 2 servings of luxuriously flavored chicken and is a traditional saffron recipe. Make some saffron rice to go with it. You will need a large skillet with a lid that covers tightly.

Ingredients:

2 boneless, skinless chicken breasts, trimmed of fat and cut into strips on a diagonal
1 tablespoon butter
1 tablespoon olive oil
1 large onion, peeled and cut lengthwise into slivers
¾ cup chicken stock
1 pinch (less than ¼ teaspoon) ground saffron
½ teaspoon sea salt
1 ½ tablespoon fresh squeezed lemon juice
¼ cup parsley, finely chopped.

Directions:

- Heat a heavy skillet over medium high heat and add the butter and olive oil to melt.

- Place the chicken in and brown on all sides but do not cook through. Remove the chicken to a plate and set aside.

- Add the onion to the skillet and brown on low heat until edges turn brown, about 12 minutes. Use a slotted spoon to remove onion to a bowl.

- Return the chicken to the skillet and cover with the onions.

- In a saucepan heat the chicken stock over medium low heat until it is hot but not boiling.

- While the stock is heating, place the saffron and salt in a mortar and pestle and grind together.

- Use about ¼ teaspoon + a pinch and add it to the chicken stock and stir so it dissolves.

- Pour the saffron liquid over the chicken and onions and bring to simmer. Once a simmer is achieved, cover with a lid and simmer over very low heat for 30 to 45 minutes.

- Add the lemon juice and parsley and simmer another 15 minutes with the lid off. If it starts to dry out, add a little more water.

- Serve over rice.

Old Recipe Sassafras Root Beer

Featuring: Sassafras

The recipe I chose to use in this book is the root beer recipe that is a little different than the one my great uncle used and a little safer. It makes 2 ½ quarts of root beer and you make a syrup with the sassafras roots. I remember going through the woods next to the fields at my grandparent's house looking for sassafras saplings, digging them up on one side and cutting off roots. You need to find ¼ inch thick roots and about 30 to 40 inches of them. We would re-plant the sapling and take the roots home to wash and chop into ½ inch pieces and the brew would begin. We did make this over a fire with a big pot on a chain and tripod because it does tend to make the whole house stink.

Ingredients:
Sassafras roots (30 or 40 inches of root, cut in ½ inch pieces)
4 cups water
2 whole cloves
½ teaspoon fennel or anise seed
4 allspice berries
1 inch stick of cinnamon
¼ cup molasses
1 cup sugar
2 drops mint extract

2 quarts soda water, cold

Directions:

- The roots are very hard so cut in ½ inch pieces with pruning shears and scrub them clean of any dirt. I use a nail brush to do this.

- Place the roots in a large heavy pan with the 4 cups of water and add the cloves, anise, allspice berries and cinnamon stick. Bring to a boil and reduce to simmer 25 minutes partially covered.

- Add the molasses and simmer 10 minutes until it dissolves and remove from heat and let cool about minutes.

- Have a large container ready to strain the liquid. Strain through cheese cloth or fine mesh lined with a paper towel on top. The liquid will still be hot. When we made it in the backyard, we used a large piece cheesecloth and placed it over a big bowl with 4 people holding on to the corners, but we made it in large quantities. You want to get any of the solids in the mixture out so you only have a clear liquid. Nothing is worse than chunky root beer.

- Clean out the pot and return the liquid to it.

- Add the sugar and heat the mixture up so the sugar dissolves and remove from the heat and let cool completely.

- While it is cooling, add the 2 drops mint extract if you want. You now have root beer syrup.

- To make the root beer, fill a glass with ice and add syrup and soda water in a 1 to 2 ratio. We would go with 1/3 cup of the syrup to 2/3 cup of soda water and that was plenty strong. You might want to tone it down or make it stronger.

Sweet and Lovely Rose Geranium Pound Cake

Featuring: Scented Geraniums

Scented geraniums come in all shapes and sizes with different colored small flowers and are scented in many different ways from nutmeg to rose to leman and all the way to citronella. They are nothing like the regular geranium with big balls of flowers. To cook, I usually use the lemon or rose flavored leaves. I have served the following pound cake at teas and it was always well received. I use rose flavored leaves but have used lemon ones on occasion as well. Make the cake in a 10-inch tube pan (not a Bundt pan) or in two medium loaf pans. I have a large loaf pan and it fits in. It makes about 15 to 16 slices.

Ingredients:

6 large rose geranium leaves, washed and dried stems removed
¾ cup butter, room temperature
8 egg whites
1 ½ cups buttermilk
2 teaspoons vanilla
4 ½ cups cake flour, sifted
¾ teaspoon baking soda
¼ teaspoon baking powder
¼ teaspoon salt

Directions:

- Coat the front sides of the geranium leaves with butter flavored non-stick spray and also spray the top and sides of the tube pan. Place the leaves, sprayed side down in the top of the tube pan and set aside.

- In a mixing bowl with electric mixer, beat the butter until creamy and gradually add the sugar.

- Add the egg whites and beat well.

- In a bowl combine the buttermilk with the vanilla and stir well.

- In another bowl combine the flour, baking soda, baking powder and salt and whisk to combine.

- Add the flour mixture alternately with the buttermilk mixture to the egg mixture beating well after each addition. Start and end with the flour mixture.

- Carefully pour the batter into the tube pan being careful not to dislodge the geranium leaves.

- Bake in a preheated 325 oven for 1 hour and 35 minutes or until a toothpick inserted in the center of the tube pan comes out clean.

- Cool 10 minutes and flip cake over onto a wire rack.

- Sprinkle with powdered sugar or make a glaze with rosewater or vanilla to drizzle over.

Easy Yet Tasty Sesame Noodle Side Dish

Featuring: Sesame Seed

Sesame seeds give extra flavor and crunch to a dish especially if you toast them. For those going through menopause, sesame seed can lessen hot flashes so eat them by the teaspoon full or just cook with them. The following recipe makes an 8 serving side dish that is spicy and crunchy because of sesame seed.

Ingredients:
1 16-ounce package linguini
4 cloves garlic, peeled and minced
6 tablespoons safflower oil
6 tablespoons granulated sugar
6 tablespoons rice vinegar
6 tablespoons soy sauce
2 tablespoons sesame oil
2 teaspoons chili sauce
6 green onions, sliced thin
2 teaspoons sesame seed, toasted

Directions:
- Cook the pasta in lightly salted water until al dente and drain. Transfer to a serving bowl and set aside.

- In a skillet over medium heat, sauté the garlic in the safflower oil for 2 minutes and add the sugar, rice vinegar, soy sauce, sesame oil and chili sauce. Bring to a boil while stirring constantly making sure the sugar dissolves.

- Pour this sauce over the linguini and toss to coat all the noodles.

- Garnish with the green onions and sesame seeds and serve.

Japanese Watermelon Shiso Salad

Featuring: Shiso

Shiso is a Japanese herb and leaf that comes in either reddish purple or green. the leaves are rich in calcium, iron and other vitamins and they do tend to prevent digestive issues. The shiso recipe I have chosen is a watermelon salad that is delicious with ribbons of shiso leaves garnishing. It is very refreshing and flavorful and feeds about 6 to 8 servings. It is very refreshing for a hot summer day.

Ingredients:
4 to 5 cups seedless watermelon, cut in 1-inch cubes
3 scallions, cut thin diagonally
1 cup cucumber, skin removed and diced
¼ cup fresh cilantro, chopped
½ teaspoon fresh ginger, peeled and finely minced
1 ½ tablespoons honey or agave nectar
1 ½ tablespoons fresh squeezed lime juice
1 tablespoon toasted sesame oil
1 ½ teaspoons light soy sauce
2 to 3 shiso leaves, rolled and cut in thin strips
2 to 3 tablespoons toasted sesame seeds

Directions:

- Place watermelon, scallions, cucumber and cilantro in a large bowl, mix and set aside.

- In a small bowl, combine the ginger, honey, lime juice, sesame oil and soy sauce and whisk until well combined.

- Pour the dressing over the watermelon mixture and gently stir to coat.

- Sprinkle with shiso ribbons and toasted sesame seed.

Spicy Turmeric and Honey Roasted Turkey

Featuring: Turmeric

Turmeric is a rich golden color and it tends to turn food that color too. It is warm and flavorful and once you try it you will want to include it in soups stews, rice dishes and more. Turn Thanksgiving around by serving a turmeric and honey glazed turkey. No one will forget this holiday feast in a long time.

Ingredients:
12 pound turkey
4 springs of rosemary
1 teaspoons thyme
1 teaspoon rubbed sage
2 teaspoons sea salt, divided
½ teaspoon black pepper
4 cups chicken broth
8 tablespoons butter, cut in slices, divided, room temperature
½ teaspoon onion powder
1 teaspoon ground turmeric
2 tablespoons honey
1 tablespoon garlic, peeled and minced

Directions:

- Thaw the turkey per package directions, remove bag of parts inside and rinse with cool water. Pat with dry paper towels and place in a roasting pan on a rack.

- Preheat the oven to 325 degrees F and move rack to the bottom.

- In a small bowl mix the thyme, sage, 1 teaspoon of the sea salt and pepper.

- Life the skin of the turkey and rub 4 tablespoons of the butter underneath and on the breast and thighs of the turkey and do the same with the herb mix in the bowl.

- Pour the broth into the bottom of the pan and roast 1 hour uncovered.

- Remove turkey from the oven and baste with the broth in the bottom of the pan. Add up to 2 more cups of broth if needed.

- Tent the turkey with aluminum foil and return to the oven. Cook, basting every 45 minutes until an internal thermometer inserted in the thigh reaches 165 degrees F.

- Melt the remaining butter in a saucepan. Stir in the remaining salt, onion powder, turmeric, honey and garlic and whisk until smooth. Use a basting brush to glaze the turkey and put back in the oven 15 minutes uncovered or until the glaze turns a lovely golden brown.

- Let the turkey sit 20 minutes before carving.

Citrus flavor is always nice to cook with and the following herbs and spices in Chapter 5
all have citrus qualities. Most are lemon flavored but there are a few that taste like
range.

Chapter 5: Delightful Citrus Flavored Herbs and Spices

It seems there are many different herbs and spices that have that fresh citrus flavor and the following recipes make very good use of them. There are recipes for jelly, cookies, sweet bread and lovely main dishes with chicken, salmon and shrimp. All of them are citrusy good.

Sweet and Delicious Cranberry Beebalm Jelly

Featuring: Beebalm

The following jelly is made with cranberries and beebalm and it is delightfully tart. This jelly is spectacular on toast and especially toast made with homemade bread. Try it on muffins too. The firework looking petals are what is used in this recipe and make sure to only use those from the red flower variety because they have more flavor. This recipe makes five 6-pint jars.

Ingredients:
½ cup water
½ cup fresh beebalm petals removed from the flower
4 cups cranberry juice
¼ cup lemon juice
1 ¾ ounce dry pectin powder
4 ½ cups sugar

Directions:

- Bring the water to a boil in a tea pot.

- Place the beebalm petals in a mug and pour the water over. Let it steep 1 hour or overnight in the refrigerator once it cools down.

- Strain and discard the petals.

- Pour the infusion into a heavy pot on the stove and add the cranberry juice and lemon juice.

- Whisk while adding the powdered pectin and keep whisking until it dissolves.

- Turn the heat to medium high and bring to a rolling boil, stirring frequently.

- Add the sugar and whisk in well. Let it boil 1 minute.

- Foam should form on the top, use a spoon or spatula to skim the foam off and discard it.

- Use a ladle to place the mixture in the sterilized jars making sure there is about ¼ inch headroom from the lip of the jar to the jelly.

- Cap the jars with rings and lids (we are using Mason Jars) and process in boiling water bath for 5 minutes. Carefully remove to a towel covered table and let cool. Be careful because the jars will be hot.

- You should hear the seal invert with a light pop while it is cooling and the lid should slope in.

- Store in the cupboard for up to 9 months (it won't last that long.

Lemony Pasta with Citrus Peel

Featuring: Citrus Peel

Want a change when making pasta? Try a lemon flavored pasta for a real treat. This recipe uses a lemon sauce made with zest and juice for a 4 serving delight. The recipe is interesting because the only thing you cook is the pasta. The sauce is fresh and not cooked. It is important you have the sauce ready when the pasta is done so that it warms the sauce.

Ingredients:
1 pound spaghetti, cooked al dente and drained
1 clove garlic, peeled and cut in half
2 lemons, room temperature, juiced
5 tablespoons olive oil

salt to taste
1 cup grated Parmesan cheese + more for garnish
1 bunch fresh parsley, chopped fine
zest of 1 of the lemons

Directions:

- Boil water for the spaghetti, add and cook until al dente and drain.

- While the spaghetti is cooking rub the halves of garlic in and around the serving bowl on the inside so it coats the surface of the bowl, Discard the rest of the garlic.

- Squeeze the lemons into the bowl.

- Drizzle the olive oil in while whisking briskly so the ingredients emulsify.

- Add the salt and Parmesan Cheese and whisk to combine.

- Add the hot drained spaghetti to the serving bowl and use two forks to mix everything in and coat the spaghetti evenly.

- Sprinkle with more Parmesan and fresh parsley.

- Add the lemon zest right before serving.

Indian Inspired Lime Leaf Soup

Featuring: Kaffir Lime

Kaffir Lime is becoming very popular as a flavoring agent in the United States these days. The leaves are what are used and fresh is the best way to cook with them. Not only are they delicious with the flavor of lime, but they are also good for the immune system. A bowl of the soup below will make you feel 100 percent better when you have a bad cold. The soup is fragrant and delicious. This recipe makes 4 to 6 servings.

Ingredients:
1 can coconut milk
3 cups vegetable stock

3 tablespoon fresh ginger, peeled and grated
3 garlic cloves, peeled and chopped
2 stalks lemongrass, peeled and pounded
5 Kaffir lime leaves
1 handful cilantro, chopped
1 handful Lemon Basil, chopped
1 tablespoon turmeric powder
3 tablespoons peanut butter
1 long chili pepper, chopped
2 tablespoons soy sauce
2 tablespoons tomato paste
2 tablespoons raw sugar
Cooked rice noodles
Fresh bean sprouts
green onion, chopped
lime wedges

Directions:

- In a large pot, place the coconut milk, stock, ginger, garlic, lemongrass, Kaffir Lime leaves and bring to a low boil. Boil 8 minutes until the lemongrass and ginger infuse into the broth.

- Add the cilantro, Thai basil, turmeric, peanut butter, chili pepper, soy sauce, tomato paste and sugar and low boil another 10 minutes.

- Remove the lemongrass stalks and Kaffir lime leaves and discard.

- Place rice noodles in a serving bowl with fresh bean sprouts and ladle the broth over top.

- Garnish with green onion and put some more Thai basil and/or cilantro over top.

- Serve with a few lime slices that can be squeezed into the broth if desired.

Buttery Lemon Balm Shortbread

Featuring: Lemon Balm

Lemon balm is very easy to grow, in fact, too easy. It will take over a garden if it isn't confined, so if you have lemon balm in your garden, you can make tons of this lovely shortbread. Shortbread is a light and buttery cookie and lends itself well to lemon flavoring. Regular shortbread dough is a bit crumbly but this dough is pliable and elastic. Because of that, I roll it out and use cookie cutters. I sprinkle each cut out with a little colored sugar.

Ingredients:
1 stick (1/2 cup) unsalted butter at room temperature
½ cup + 1 tablespoon powdered sugar
1 teaspoon lemon zest
1/8 teaspoon salt
1 cup all-purpose flour
3 tablespoons lemon balm, washed, dried and chopped fine

Directions:

- Beat the butter and powder sugar together in a mixer.

- Add the powder sugar slowly. Follow with the lemon zest and salt. Beat well.

- Add the flour gradually and a slow speed. The dough will be thick and you might have to use your hands to incorporate all the flour.

- Add the lemon balm and mix in with the mixer, if you can, or with your hands. Avoid touching the dough as much as possible because it will make it tough.

- Form the dough into a ball, wrap in plastic wrap and put it in the refrigerator about 20 minutes.

- Roll the dough out on floured wax paper and use cookie cutters to cut out shapes.

- Put the shapes on a cookie sheet 1 inch apart and sprinkle colored sugar on top.

- Bake in a preheated 350 degree F oven for 8 to 10 minutes or until the start to brown on the edges.

- Cool on the cookie sheet about 5 minutes and remove and cool on racks.

Lemony Butter Basil Chicken in a Skillet

Featuring: Lemon Basil

Lemon basil has the same spicy basil flavor mixed with a bit of lemon. Anything lemon flavored is good when you have a cold, but lemon basil gives you some extra healing power and strengthens the immune system. The following chicken recipe will impress your family and friends, even if they don't have a cold, and it very easy to make. You will get 4 servings and want more.

Ingredients:
1 ½ cups chicken broth
3 tablespoons fresh squeezed lemon juice
1 teaspoon dried lemon basil leaves or 1 tablespoon fresh, chopped
3 tablespoons cornstarch
2 tablespoons butter, divided
4 bone-in chicken thighs with skin on
¼ teaspoon salt
1/8 teaspoon pepper
2 teaspoons garlic, peeled and chopped

Directions:
- Preheat the oven to 400 degrees F.

- In a glass 4 cup measuring cup, combine the chicken broth, lemon juice, lemon basil leaves and cornstarch and whisk until blended.

- In a large ovenproof skillet over medium high heat, melt 1 tablespoon of the butter and salt and pepper all sides of the chicken thighs. Place the chicken in the butter about 5 to 10 minutes turning once to brown all sides. Transfer to a plate and keep warm.

- Reduce heat to medium low and melt the remaining 1 tablespoon of butter in the same skillet. Stir in the broth mixture and add the garlic. Cook about 5 minutes, stirring until the sauce thickens a bit.

- Return the chicken to the skillet and put in the oven for 15 to 20 minutes or until the chicken is done and the internal temperature is 165 degrees F.

Asian Inspired Lemongrass Garlic Shrimp

Featuring: Lemongrass

I find lemongrass hard to work with because the stalks are very strong and rigid and you have to get to the soft middle of the stalk. It is worth all the hammering and work though because the flavor is exceptional. This recipe is a little easier because you use all the stalk and chop it in a food processor. The outer part of lemongrass is not good to eat and can cause problems in the digestive system, but in this recipe, you only use the lemongrass as a marinade and discard it when the shrimp are done marinating. The following recipe is based off Tom Yung soup without the chilis and made into a main dish. I often serve this dish with rice that was cooked with lemongrass. This recipe makes 4 servings.

Ingredients:
2 tablespoons fish sauce
3 tablespoons vegetable oil
¼ cup sugar
1 lemongrass stalk, trimmed, peeled and cut in several large pieces
2 cloves garlic, peeled and grated
36 jumbo tiger shrimp, peeled and deveined (approximately 2 pounds)

Directions:

- Place the fish sauce, vegetable oil, sugar, inner soft part of the lemongrass and garlic into a food processor or chopper. Process until the lemongrass is chopped very fine.

- Place the shrimp in a large re-closable plastic bag and pour the sauce over top. Marinate in the refrigerator about 45 minutes to 1 hour.

- While marinating, set your grill to high heat.

- Remove the shrimp to a plate and discard the marinade.

- Load 6 shrimp onto a 12-inch skewer and place on grill rack.

- Grill 2 minutes each side or until the shrimp are done all the way through.

- Serve with rice.

Lemon Thyme Chicken in Creamy Citrus Sauce

Featuring: Lemon Thyme

Lemon thyme is a very pretty plant and looks lovely in a pot on your front porch. The leaves are green with yellow or white margins and they taste like thyme with just a little bit of citrus flavor. The following lemon sauce is good on chicken and is very creamy and rich. The recipe only takes 30 short minutes to make and will be gobbled up quickly. The recipe makes 4 creamy lemon flavored servings.

Ingredients:
2 teaspoons fresh lemon thyme, chopped
1 teaspoon garlic powder
1 teaspoon lemon pepper
½ teaspoon sea salt
2 teaspoons Italian seasoning
4 boneless skinless chicken breasts
1 tablespoon olive oil
1 teaspoon garlic, peeled and minced
½ cup mushrooms, cleaned and sliced
½ cup chicken broth

2 tablespoons fresh squeezed lemon juice (about 1 lemon)
1 cup heavy cream

Directions:

- In a bowl, combine the lemon thyme, garlic powder, lemon pepper, sea salt and Italian seasoning and whisk well.

- Sprinkle half of the above mixture on both sides of each chicken breast.

- Heat a large skillet to medium high and add the olive oil.

- Add the chicken breasts and lower the heat to medium low cooking chicken about 5 to 7 minutes on each side or until brown and cooked all the way through.

- Remove chicken to a plate and keep warm.

- In the same skillet over medium heat, sauté the garlic and mushrooms about 2 to 3 minutes or until mushrooms are tender.

- Add the chicken broth, lemon juice and remaining seasoning mixture.

- Stir in the cream and whisk, brining the mixture to a boil. Continue to whisk and boil 2 to 3 minutes as the sauce thickens.

- Remove from heat and return the chicken to the skillet coating all sides with the sauce.

- Garnish with lemon slices and more fresh lemon thyme.

Strongly Citrus Verbena Tea Bread

Featuring: Lemon Verbena

I grow a lemon verbena plant every summer in a pot on my porch and harvest the leave in July and when it starts to get cold. Unfortunately, the plant will not survive 40 degree temperatures, but I usually get enough leaves to dry to make tea all winter and use it in recipes. Lemon verbena is a strong lemon flavor that does not diminish when dried. I still have some dried leaves from two years ago and they are still lemony fresh. This delicious lemon tea bread is baked in a regular loaf pan and yields 8 to 10 slices of lemony deliciousness. It actually is more like a sweet cake than sweet bread.

Ingredients:
½ cup milk (whole or 2%)
10 Lemon verbena leaves (whole)
½ cup butter, room temperature
¾ cup granulated sugar
2 eggs
1 ½ cups all-purpose flour
1 teaspoon baking powder
½ teaspoon salt
1 tablespoon grated lemon zest
2 tablespoons lemon verbena leaves, chopped (about 20)
3 tablespoons fresh squeezed lemon juice
1 cup powdered sugar
A few more leaves for decorating

Directions:

- In a saucepan over medium low heat, combine the milk and whole lemon verbena leaves. Stir occasionally and bring it to steaming but not to a boil. Once it steams, cool to room temperature.

- Once the mixture is cool, strain to remove the verbena leaves and measure. If there is not ½ cup, add a little more milk.

- Preheat the oven to 350 degrees F and prepare an 8x4 inch loaf pan by greasing and flouring it.

- Beat the softened butter in a mixer bowl with an electric mixture until it is creamy. Gradually add granulated sugar until fluffy, about 2 minutes.

- Add eggs, beating well after each one.

- In another bowl, combine the flour, baking powder and salt. Add it in 3 installments alternating with the milk mixture beating on low after each addition. Begin and end with flour mixture.

- Stir the lemon zest in by hand and spoon batter into the prepared loaf pan.

- Bake for 1 hour or until a toothpick inserted into the center comes out clean. Cool in the pan 10 minutes and turnout on to a wire rack.

- While cooling, mix the chopped verbena leaves and lemon juice in a small bowl. Cover and set aside until the bread has cooled.

- Once cooled, strain out the lemon juice and discard the lemon verbena leaves. Whisk in the powdered sugar adding a little more lemon juice if needed. This needs to be drizzled over the bread.

- Take a chop stick or skewer and carefully poke 8 to 10 holes in the top of the bread.

- Spoon the glaze over top and let it drip down the sides. It will also drip down the holes and give some, almost syrupy moistness to the top of the bread.

- Cut and serve.

Creamy Mexican Tortilla Soup

Featuring: Mexican Oregano

Mexican oregano has a lovely citrus flavor and is exceptional in a tortilla soup. The following recipe is for Tortilla soup that you can use regular oregano, but the Mexican oregano gives it a brighter flavor. This makes 6 to 8 servings.

Ingredients:
2 tablespoons olive oil
2 onions, peeled and chopped
½ green bell pepper, seeded and diced
3 cloves garlic, peeled and chopped
2 tablespoons soy sauce

¼ teaspoon smoked Spanish paprika

2 teaspoons green chili powder (I use red if I can't find green and it is fine)

2 teaspoons ground cumin

1 ½ teaspoons Mexican oregano

1 teaspoon sea salt

8 cups vegetable or chicken broth

1/3 cup tomato paste

1 28 ounce can diced tomatoes (juice and all)

¼ teaspoon liquid smoke (optional)

8 6-inch corn tortillas cut in strips

Directions:

- Heat the oil in a stock pot over medium heat and add the onion, peppers and garlic and sauté about 5 minutes.

- Stir in the soy sauce, paprika, chili powder, cumin Mexican oregano and salt and stir cooking 2 minutes.

- Add the broth, tomato paste, tomatoes and liquid smoke and bring everything to simmer. Cover and simmer 15 minutes.

- Use a blender or immersion blender to blend the soup smooth and serve with warmed tortilla strips on top and sour cream.

Savory Salmon with Butter Herb and Sorrel Sauce

Featuring: Sorrel

Use sorrel with fatty meats and fish because it breaks that fat down to be more digestible. This recipe does just that with salmon. Before beginning, place the salmon on a cutting board and cut into 16 pieces on an angle. The piece will be small, but each person will get several. lace the pieces on a parchment lined baking sheet until ready to cook.

Ingredients:

1 pound salmon, cut in 16 medallions

Olive oil
salt and pepper to taste
3 tablespoons butter, room temperature
¼ cup fresh chervil, chopped
½ cup fresh chives, chopped
2 cups fresh sorrel, chopped
½ cup heavy cream

Directions:

- Warm the plates you will be using for the salmon. I put my oven proof plates in my toaster oven on low heat or in the dishwasher under the heat cycle.

- After cutting the medallions, brush them with olive oil and season with salt and pepper. Place on parchment lined baking sheet, skin side up.

- Set aside and turn the broiler on high and wait for it to heat up.

- In a large skillet, melt the butter and let it start to turn golden brown.

- Place the salmon medallions in the broiler and let it broil 2 to 3 minutes but be careful to watch, it might take less time for it to be done.

- Back in the skillet, add the chervil, chives and sorrel and allow the herbs to wilt.

- Pour in the cream and bring to a boil. Reduce heat immediately and stir. Once the creamy mixture coats the back of a spoon, it is done.

- Remove the plates from warmer and dry off. Place 4 medallions on a plate and drizzle with the sauce evenly.

- Serve immediately.

Roasted Spicy Sumac Chickpea Dish

Featuring: Sumac

Sumac berries are very sour, kind of like a juiceless lemon and they make a dish very bright. The following dish is vegetarian using chickpeas and a host of other spices and herbs. The chickpeas are roasted with this coating and can be used as a very delicious citrus flavored snack.

Ingredients:

2 14 ounce cans chickpeas, rinsed and drained
2 tablespoons olive oil
1 teaspoon cayenne pepper
1 teaspoon paprika
2 teaspoons sumac
½ teaspoon sea salt
¼ teaspoon ground pepper
½ teaspoon ground cumin

Directions:

- Preheat the oven to 425 degrees F and line a baking sheet with a rim with parchment paper.

- Place the chickpeas in a clean towel and gently press and roll around to absorb all the moisture from them.

- In a large bowl, combine the olive oil, cayenne, paprika, sumac, salt, pepper and cumin and whisk well.

- Add the dried chickpeas and toss well to coat.

- Pour onto the prepared baking pan and arrange in a single layer.

- Roast 15 minutes, shake the pan and turn it and roast another 10 minutes. The chickpeas should be lightly browned and crispy when done and it may take another 5 or 10 minutes.

- Serve warm or store in an airtight container room temperature.

Exotic Orange Glazed Tamarind Chicken

Featuring: Tamarind

The following recipe is an orange flavored chicken dish that is so bright it will be hard to go back to regular chicken. The recipe uses tamarind paste that is easily found in the world section of large grocery stores or in Indian food stores. The recipe says to marinate the chicken 1 to 6 hours. I put mine in to marinade before work and 8 hours seems to be just the right amount of time. The recipe makes 4 servings.

Ingredients:
¼ cup olive oil
2 large cloves garlic, peeled and chopped
2 tablespoons Herbs de Provence
¼ teaspoon salt
1/8 teaspoon pepper
4 boneless, skinless chicken breast halves
2 tablespoons unsalted butter, melted
1 14.5 ounce can low sodium chicken broth
¾ cup fresh squeezed orange juice
zest of the orange
¼ cup white sugar
2 tablespoons tamarind paste
1 tablespoon fresh ginger, grated
1 dash Sriracha sauce

Directions:
- In a shallow bowl, whisk the olive oil, garlic, Herbs de Province, salt and pepper and place the chicken in to cover. Cover with plastic wrap and place in the refrigerator 1 to 6 hours.

- Preheat or start your grill to get it hot.

- In a large skillet, melt the butter and add the chicken broth, orange juice, orange zest, sugar, tamarind paste, and ginger. Whisk to combine well.

- Bring to a boil over medium high heat whisking often until the mixture has reduced to about ¾ cup and coats the back of a spoon. This should take about 25 to 30 minutes.

- Remove the glaze from the heat and add the Sriracha sauce and taste to see if it needs more salt or pepper.

- Spray a grill pan with non-stick spray and pour 3 tablespoons of the glaze in a small bowl to baste the chicken once it starts to cook.

- Remove the chicken breasts from the marinade and discard. Place on the grill and cook until done, about 4 minutes each side, basting with the glaze in the bowl every once in a while.

- When the chicken is done, transfer to a plate and pour the rest of the sauce over top and serve hot.

Vietnamese Coriander Fish and Red Curry

Featuring: Vietnamese Coriander

This chicken salad recipe is a little different from what you might be used to. I serve it in a bowl and not between two pieces of bread. Make it from left over chicken that has already been cooked. The French fried onions are the kind you get in a paper can at the grocery store. This recipe makes 4 servings.

Ingredients:
3 cups cooked chicken, cut in bite size pieces
1 cup Vietnamese coriander leaves, roughly chopped
Juice of 1 lime
4 green onions, sliced thin
1 teaspoon fish sauce
1 tablespoon oil (vegetable, olive oil or my favorite-grape seed oil)
¼ cup French fried onions
Romain lettuce leaves (optional)

Directions:

- Remove any fat or skin from the chicken before cutting into bite size pieces and place the pieces in a bowl. The chicken should be cold.

- Add the chopped Vietnamese coriander to the bowl with the chicken.

- Combine the lime juice, onions, fish sauce and oil in a small bowl and whisk together well.

- Pour over the chicken and toss to coat all the chicken pieces.

- Sprinkle with the French fried onions on top.

- Either eat with a fork or take Romain lettuce leaves, scoop out some of the chicken salad into the leaves, roll and eat.

Chapter 6 is for those that love hot and spicy foods. This chapter will get your tongue
tingling and your brow sweating but it will be a lovely experience. Use cayenne, curry,
pepper, paprika and more to make deliciously zingy recipes.

Chapter 6: Hot and Fiery Herbs and Spices

I like a little spice with my food but I consider myself a mild spice lover. I have friends that like to make themselves sweat when they eat. These herbs and spices do have the ability to do that, but they can also be tamed down to give food zing without breathing fire. Hot and fiery herbs are good for your health. They get circulation going by dilating blood vessels and making things move through easily. Believe it or not, some of them actually enhance digestion too. The following recipes do include those that will make you sweat and breathe fire to those that have a delightful kick.

Luscious Burgers with Cayenne Bourbon Sauce

Featuring: Cayenne

Cayenne, beef and bourbon mix to make some of the best hamburgers ever made. They are sweet and hot and you don't notice you are sweating because they are so delicious. Making cayenne bourbon burgers on a hot day will make even 90 degree weather feel cool. This makes 4 burgers.

Ingredients:
1 pound ground beef
1 egg, beaten
½ cup breadcrumbs
shredded cheddar
1 cup tomato juice
1 cup pineapple juice
¼ cup honey
1 clove garlic, peeled and crushed
1 tablespoon steak sauce
1 tablespoon Dijon mustard
½ to 1 teaspoon cayenne powder
¼ cup bourbon
2 tablespoons cornstarch
2 tablespoons water
4 buns

Directions:

- In a large bowl, mix the ground beef, egg and breadcrumbs. Form into 4 patties and set aside until they reach room temperature.

- Heat a grill to medium high.

- While the grill is heating, place in a saucepan, the tomato juice, pineapple juice, honey, garlic, steak sauce, mustard and cayenne. Stir and slowly bring to a simmer.

- Slowly add the bourbon and stir. Bring to a boil and boil 2 minutes stirring constantly.

- Reduce heat to a simmer and mix the cornstarch and water in a small bowl to make a paste. Pour it into the sauce and let it thicken. This will happen quickly. Remove from heat.

- Grill the burgers to desired doneness and let rest on a plate for 3 to 5 minutes.

- Place a burger on each bun and brush liberally with the sauce.

- Serve immediately.

Tex-Mex Hot Chicken Tacos

Featuring: Chili Powder

Tex-Mex food is traditionally hot and spicy and the following chicken tacos are no different. The following recipe is for a delicious chicken chili taco filling that your family will not be able to get enough of. Serve with salsa, chopped lettuce, chopped tomatoes, shredded cheese and sour cream. This recipe makes about 4 big servings.

Ingredients:
1 pound boneless, skinless chicken breasts, cut in thin strips
1 teaspoon chili powder
½ teaspoon cumin
1 teaspoon garlic powder

½ teaspoon salt
1 tablespoon olive oil
4 8 inch flour tortillas
Condiments

Directions:

- Cut the strips of chicken and place in a bowl.

- In a small bowl, combine the chili powder, cumin, garlic powder and salt and whisk to combine well.

- Pour over the chicken and toss so that all strips are seasoned well.

- Place a large skillet over medium high heat and add the olive oil.

- Add the chicken strips, a little at a time and sauté cooking until cooked through. Remove to a platter and continue with the rest of the strips when done.

- Serve on the tortillas with toppings.

Wilted Salad with Roasted Zesty Cumin

Featuring: Cumin

Cumin is delightfully spicy and it might make your metabolism run faster and help you to lose weight. Not only that, but it also helps with digestive issues. I thought I would give you a different recipe using cumin than a curry. This is a nice side dish using cabbage and it makes 6 servings.

Ingredients:
1 teaspoon cumin seed
2 teaspoon olive oil
12 cups coarsely chopped Savoy cabbage (about 2 pounds)
½ cup water
½ teaspoon salt
¼ teaspoon pepper
1 tablespoon sherry vinegar

Directions:

- Place a non-stick skillet over medium heat and add the cumin seeds and heat and stir 1 minute or until they become fragrant. Shake and stir pan frequently. Pour into a small bowl and set aside.

- Put the oil in the same skillet over medium heat and add the cabbage and water. Cook 6 minutes until the cabbage starts to wilt stirring occasionally.

- Sprinkle over the salt and pepper and stir.

- Pour the seeds into the cabbage mixture along with the vinegar and cook on low for about 5 minutes, stirring frequently until heated through.

Curried Coconut Chicken

Featuring: Curry

Curry is a blend of spices that make for a flavorful ally in the kitchen. Most of the components promote cardiac health and may help in digesting fatty foods. The following recipe uses curry powder infused in vegetable oil to make a wonderful and tasty chicken dish. The recipe makes 6 servings that can be served with curry powder infused rice.

Ingredients:
2 pounds boneless, skinless chicken breasts pounded, cut in ½ inch chunks
1 teaspoon salt
1 teaspoon pepper
1 ½ tablespoons vegetable oil
2 tablespoons curry powder
½ onion, peeled and thinly sliced
2 cloves garlic, peeled and crushed
1 14 ounce can coconut milk
1 14.5 ounce can diced tomatoes
1 8-ounce can tomato sauce

3 tablespoons sugar

Directions:

- Season the chicken with salt and pepper on both sides and set aside.

- Heat the vegetable oil in a skillet over medium high heat and add the curry powder. Stir vigorously for about 1 minute.

- Add the onions and garlic and sauté 1 minute.

- Add the chicken breast chunks moving around to coat. Reduce to medium and cook and cook about 7 minutes, stirring frequently.

- Pour in the coconut milk, tomatoes, tomato sauce and sugar and stir.

- Cover and simmer, stirring occasionally about 30 minutes and serve over rice.

Horseradish Crusted Roast Beef

Featuring: Horseradish

Horseradish is a main component in shrimp sauce and is hot and spicy on a roast beef sandwich. If you have a cold, horseradish will make your nose and sinuses run so that everything clears. It is an antioxidant and anti-inflammatory and helps heal infections of every kind. The following recipe is very delicious and makes 8 to 10 servings of a horseradish encrusted roast.

Ingredients:
1 6 pound sirloin tip roast
½ cup prepared horseradish
2 tablespoons kosher salt
2 tablespoons Dijon mustard
2 tablespoons fresh parsley, chopped
1 tablespoon ground black pepper
1 tablespoon granulated sugar
1 tablespoon sherry vinegar

Directions:

- Preheat the oven to 375 degrees F and put a rack in a large roasting pan with the roast on top.

- In a small bowl, mix the horseradish, salt, mustard, parsley pepper and sugar. Whisk well.

- Add the vinegar to make a thick paste and slater on the top of the roast and down the sides.

- Roast for 2 hours or until the internal temperature of the roast is 125 degrees F.

- Place on a cutting board to rest 15 minutes and cover with foil to keep warm.

- Slice thin against the grain.

Nasturtium and Delectable Cream Cheese Tea Sandwiches

Featuring: Nasturtium

Nasturtiums are a very pretty climbing flower. I have them climbing up my outdoor lamppost and they have such sunny colors. The leaves and the flowers are also peppery flavored and make great additions to salad. Tea sandwiches are fun to make and eat at a formal tea and nasturtiums mixed with cream cheese and sour cream make for some delicious snacks. Serve these with herbal teas in the garden.

Ingredients:
8 slices of bread (you choose what kind you like)
8 ounces cream cheese, softened
2 tablespoons sour cream
12 Nasturtium blossoms, chopped
Nasturtium leaves

Directions:

- Remove the crust from the bread.

- In a bowl, combine the cream cheese and sour cream until well mixed.

- Add the chopped blossoms and mix in.

- Spread thinly on the slices of bread and cut into quarters.

- Line a plate with nasturtium leaves and arrange the sandwiches on top. Garnish with some full flowers and serve.

Old World Chicken Paprikash

Featuring: Paprika

If you have eye issues, paprika is a spice you need to consume. It stops cellular damage to the eye. The following recipe is a very good Hungarian Paprikash recipe that uses Hungarian paprika and makes about 6 servings. The original recipe uses lard, but I changed that to butter. Don't skimp on this recipe and use fat free anything, because it won't be nearly as good. This is one of those things you only eat on occasion because there is a lot of calories and fat.

Ingredients:
2 tablespoons butter at room temperature
3 pounds chicken pieces (this can be bone in and with skin)
2 yellow onions, peeled and finely chopped
2 cloves garlic, peeled and crushed
2 Roma tomatoes, seeds removed and diced
1 Hungarian bell pepper, seeded and chopped (I use a red bell pepper)
3 to 4 tablespoons sweet Hungarian paprika
2 cups chicken broth
1 ½ teaspoon sea salt
½ teaspoon ground black pepper
3 tablespoons flour
¾ cup full fat sour cream (this is something you want all the fat for)
¼ cup heavy whipping cream

Directions:

- Heat the butter in a heavy pot and add the chicken browning it on all sides. Remove the chicken to a plate.

- In the same pot, sauté the onions until golden brown, about 3 minutes.

- Add the garlic and tomatoes and sauté about 3 minutes.

- Remove from the heat and add the paprika, salt and pepper.

- Put the chicken back in the pot and turn on over medium heat.

- Pour in the broth that should almost cover the chicken pieces. Bring to a boil, reduce, cover and simmer 40 minutes.

- Remove the chicken to a plate.

- In a small bowl mix the flour into the sour cream and heavy cream to make a thick paste. Stir into the sauce and whisk to prevent lumps. Simmer until sauce thickens, about 2 to 3 minutes.

- Return the chicken to the pan and heat through.

- Serve with a dollop of sour cream.

Sweet and Spicy Holiday German Pfeffernusse Cookies

Featuring: Pepper

The recipe below is for German Pfeffernusse cookies that are delightful spice cookies shaped in a flattened ball and covered in powdered sugar. One of the ingredients is black pepper along with a host of other spices. The pepper combines well with everything else to make just a bit fierier flavor in the cookies. This recipe makes about 3 dozen pfeffernusse.

Ingredients:
½ cup molasses

½ cup brown sugar
¼ cup butter, softened
2 eggs
2 teaspoons fresh orange zest
3 cups flour
½ teaspoon ground black pepper
½ teaspoon ground cinnamon
¼ teaspoon ground anise
¼ teaspoon baking soda
½ to 1 cup powder sugar

Directions:

- In a mixing bowl, cream the molasses, brown sugar and butter until smooth.

- Add the eggs and orange zest beating in well until creamy and light.

- In a bowl whisk the flour, pepper, cinnamon, anise and baking soda until well combined. Add gradually to the wet mixture in the mixing bowl.

- The dough will be sticky but should be able to form into a ball. Place the ball in plastic wrap and put in the refrigerator overnight. This allows the spices to marinate and give the cookies more flavor.

- Preheat the oven to 350 degrees F.

- Shape the dough into 1 inch balls and place 2 inches apart on a baking sheet covered with parchment paper and sprayed with non-stick spray. Lightly press down on the balls to slightly flatten.

- Bake 12 to 15 minutes or until the cookies are puffing and slightly firm to the touch.

- Remove from baking sheet and put on racks to cool about 10 minutes.

- Pour the powdered sugar into a brown lunch bag and drop in 2 to 3 cookies at a time and flip them once or twice until they are coated with the powder sugar. The cookies should still be warm but not hot.

- Return the cookies to the rack and let them cool completely.

- The cookies will stay fresh in an airtight container for up to a week.

Fiery Red Pepper Parmesan Broccoli

Featuring: Red Pepper Flakes

I use red pepper flakes, just a few, in many of my recipes including hamburgers and meatloaf, but I really enjoy the flavor of them in vegetable dishes. The recipe below makes 4 side servings and it makes your mouth tingle with fiery delight. Roasted broccoli is good on its own but putting red pepper flakes on it makes it even better. You will be using frozen broccoli that can get a little soggy. The trick is to have the oven and pan hot before putting the dish in the oven. It won't come out soggy that way.

Ingredients:
2 tablespoons olive oil
¼ teaspoon garlic powder
¼ teaspoon red pepper flakes
¼ teaspoon salt
¼ teaspoon pepper
16 ounces frozen broccoli, thawed and drained
¼ cup Parmesan cheese

Directions:
- In a large bowl, mix the olive oil, garlic powder, red pepper flakes, salt and pepper.

- Add the broccoli that should still be frozen and toss to coat all the broccoli pieces.

- Sprinkle with Parmesan and toss again.

- Preheat the oven to 425 degrees F and wait 8 minutes.

- Place a baking sheet lined with parchment paper in the oven, with nothing on it and leave it there 5 minutes.

- Remove the baking sheet and spread the broccoli on in a single layer.

- Put it back in the oven and bake for 16 to 18 minutes or until the broccoli is browned and hot all the way through, but not burned.

- Remove from oven and serve right away.

Impressive Chocolate Wasabi Brownies

Featuring: Wasabi

I bet you didn't think I would give you a brownie recipe made with wasabi. This recipe uses crushed wasabi peas (dried chickpeas with wasabi coating) as a topping and it is delicious. Who knew wasabi and chocolate went so well together? This recipe makes 16 brownies. Use chunks of bittersweet chocolate and milk chocolate or use bittersweet chocolate and milk chocolate chips chopped up a bit.

Ingredients:
2 sticks unsalted butter, room temperature
6 ounces bittersweet chocolate, chopped
3 ounces milk chocolate, chopped
1 cup sugar
4 eggs
¾ cup flour
½ teaspoon salt
3 cups powdered sugar
¼ cup milk
1/3 cup semi-sweet chocolate chips
4 tablespoons wasabi peas

Directions:
- Preheat the oven to 350 degrees F and butter or grease an 8 inch square baking dish.

- In a bowl placed over a pan of simmering water or in a double boiler, pour in the bittersweet and milk chocolate pieces and stir constantly with a wooden spoon so they start to melt.

- Add 1 stick of the butter and let it melt together with the chocolate stirring constantly.

- Remove the bowl from the heat and let it cool 15 minutes.

- Use a whisk to incorporate the sugar and then the eggs, one egg at a time.

- Add the flour and salt and switch to a rubber spatula to fold the ingredients all together until well combined.

- Pour in the prepared baking dish and bake for 40 minutes.

- Cool completely, cut into squares and remove from the pan placing them on a wire rack.

- In a small pot over simmering water, pour in the semi-sweet chocolate chips and stir constantly until they are melted and smooth.

- Remove from heat and let cool about 10 minutes.

- n an electric mixer bowl, beat the other stick of butter until it becomes smooth.

- Add the powdered sugar and milk and beat about 1 minute.

- Pour in the melted chocolate and beat until creamy. Spread this frosting on each brownie.

- Place the wasabi peas in a small bag and seal it shut. Use a rolling pin or mallet to crush them into crumbs. Sprinkle the wasabi peas over the frosting and serve.

Not Your Grandma's Macaroni and Cheese

Featuring: White Pepper

White pepper is normally used so that you don't find black specs in light colored foods like eggs and macaroni and cheese. However, many chefs say the flavor is stronger than black pepper and some say it is the same. You be the judge. The following

111

recipe is for macaroni and cheese and uses white pepper. This is no normal mac and cheese, however. It is hot because you use white pepper, hot pepper sauce and pepper jack cheese to make it along with a little chili powder. This recipe makes 8 servings.

Ingredients:

1 ½ cups pasta (use shells, rotelles or regular old elbows)
4 tablespoons butter, divided
¼ cup flour
3 cups whole milk
1 teaspoon dry mustard
½ teaspoon salt
½ teaspoon white pepper
3 teaspoons hot pepper sauce
1 cup shredded pepper jack cheese
1 ½ cups shredded sharp Cheddar cheese
½ cup grated Parmesan cheese
½ cup breadcrumbs
2 teaspoons chili powder.

Directions:

- Preheat the oven to 375 degrees F.

- Add pasta to a pot of boiling water and cook 8 to 10 minutes or until the pasta is al dente. Drain well.

- Melt 2 tablespoons of the butter in a large, heavy saucepan over medium heat. Whisk in the flour and stir while cooking for about 1 minute. The flour should turn off white.

- Whisk in the some of the milk, some of the mustard, some of the salt, some of the white pepper and some of the hot sauce. Repeat until everything is whisked in and smooth.

- Bring to a gentle boil while stirring constantly and let it boil 1 minute. Remove from the heat and whisk in the pepper jack, Cheddar and Parmesan cheese until it is smooth.

- Pour in the drained, cooked pasta and stir so that all the pasta is coated with the cheese. Pour into a 2 quart baking dish.

- In another small pan, melt the rest of the butter and stir in the breadcrumbs with the chili powder. Sprinkle this over the macaroni and cheese in the baking dish and bake in the oven for 30 minutes. It should be bubbly when taken out. Let sit 10 minutes before serving.

I've ended the book on a sweet note with all the herbs and spices that give a lovely
sweet and spicy flavor to foods. Indulge in cinnamon, nutmeg, cloves and more to make
sweet and spicy main dishes, side dishes and desserts.

Chapter 7: Sweet and Spicy Herbs and Spices

In this chapter you will find all kinds of desserts and some holiday main dishes and treats. You will also find many barbeque recipes and other main dish suggestions. Try a holiday clove studded ham with glaze or gingery beef stir fry and then go for German potato salad or a nice jerk chicken. These sweet recipes are sure to delight anyone that eats them and they also do have some health benefits involved.

Quick and Easy Jamaican Jerk Chicken Legs

Featuring: Allspice

Just the scent of allspice is said to have a positive effect on nervousness and anxiety and if you make the following recipe for Jamaican Jerk Chicken Legs, you will find out what I mean. How can you be negative when the food tastes and smells so good? The recipe uses 2 teaspoons of ground allspice, which you can grind yourself or just use ready ground spice. The recipe calls for chicken legs, but you can also use wings. The recipe directs you to make a rub and put it on the legs and bake them in the oven.

Ingredients:
10 chicken legs
2 tablespoons brown sugar
1 tablespoon dried thyme
2 teaspoons smoked paprika
2 teaspoons ground allspice
1 teaspoon ground cloves
1 teaspoon ground cinnamon
1 teaspoon ground ginger
1 teaspoon sea salt
¼ teaspoon ground pepper
1/3 cup olive oil

Directions:

- Preheat the oven to 425 degrees F and place one rack in the middle.

- Dry the chicken of excess moisture with paper towels and use a fork to prick holes on all sides. Place on a plate and set aside.

- In a small bowl combine the brown sugar, thyme, paprika, allspice, cloves, cinnamon, ginger, salt and pepper and whisk well.

- Add the olive oil and stir to make a pasty rub.

- Rub all over the legs placing on a foil lined rimmed baking sheet with a little space between pieces. Make sure to use all the rub.

- Bake 35 to 40 minutes or until brown and fragrant. Serve hot.

Delightful Angelica Seed Pound Cake

Featuring: Angelica

You don't come across angelica often, so when you do, jump at the chance to make something with it. It is another herb that is good for relieving stress and also calms the stomach. The following recipe is a lovely angelica seed pound cake that comes from my Great Aunt that lived in England. She would top each slice with a little whipped cream and a small stalk of candied angelica. It is made in a loaf pan that is greased well and floured.

Ingredients:
1 cup granulated sugar
8 ounces unsalted butter at room temperature
1 tablespoon orange zest
1 tablespoon lemon zest
1 teaspoon vanilla extract
1 pinch Kosher salt
5 tablespoons angelica seed, toasted and ground
1 cup almond meal
4 eggs + 1 yolk

1 cup cake flour, sifted

Directions:

- In a mixer cream the sugar and butter well until light and fluffy.

- Add the orange zest, lemon zest and vanilla extract and mix to combine.

- In a small bowl, combine the salt, angelica seed and almond meal and whisk to combine. Slowly add to the ingredients in the mixer bowl until just mixed.

- Add the eggs and yolk, one at a time, beating after each addition ending with the yolk.

- Remove the bowl from the mixer and hand mix in the cake flour until well combined.

- Spread the mixture in the greased loaf pan and put in a preheated 300 degree F oven for 45 minutes to 1 hour or until a toothpick inserted in the center of the cake comes out clean.

- Cool on a rack for 15 minutes, run a knife around the edges of the loaf pan and turn out onto a rack to cool completely.

- Serve with whipped cream and candied angelica stalk.

Cool Anise Italian Wedding Cookies

Featuring: Anise

I look forward to Christmas every year because we make Italian Wedding cookies and tons of them. They freeze well, so I start in October and freeze unfrosted. There is a method to frosting these little gems. We make a thick glaze with powdered sugar and water adding some food coloring and a little anise extract in a bowl. The cookie is held in the hand right side up and dipped upside down with a little twist as it is brought out of the icing. The cookie is placed right side up on wax paper to dry an hour or so and then packed away in an airtight container until ready to serve. Anise calms an upset stomach and also stops bloating. This recipe makes 26 cookies but can be doubled and even tripled if you live in my house.

Ingredients:
½ cup unsalted butter, at room temperature
½ cup granulated sugar
3 eggs
¼ cup milk (use whole or 2%)
1 teaspoon anise extract
½ teaspoon vanilla extract
3 ¼ cup flour, divided
1 tablespoon baking powder
2 cups powdered sugar
¼ teaspoon salt
3 tablespoons water
¼ teaspoon anise extract
Sprinkles and food coloring (optional)

Directions:

- In a mixer bowl with an electric mixer, cream the butter and sugar together.

- Add the eggs and beat until light and frothy.

- Add the milk, anise and vanilla extract and beat well.

- In another bowl, combine 3 cups of the flour, baking powder and salt and whisk until combined.

- Add the flour mixture gradually to the mixer bowl and mix to make a very sticky dough. If it is too sticky add up to ¼ cup more flour. It should hold together to make a smooth ball.

- Scoop out 1 ½ inch balls and place on a cookie sheet covered with parchment paper about 1 inch apart.

- Bake 10 to 12 minutes or until lightly brown. Remove to a rack and let sit a few minutes, then remove and place on racks to cool.

- Once cool make the glaze by combining the powdered sugar, water and ¼ teaspoon anise extract. Dip and frost and sprinkle sprinkles on top. Let harden about an hour before serving or store in an airtight container until time to serve.

Refreshing Anise Hyssop Quick Bread

Featuring: Anise Hyssop

Quick breads are a wonderful invention that had to be invented by someone that had unexpected company and had to find something quick to make and serve them. This quick bread has a lovely anise flavor and I serve it with either cold or hot anise hyssop tea with infused honey. If you had a cold, it would clear it up for awhile quite deliciously. This recipe makes 1 loaf.

Ingredients:
2 cups unbleached flour
¼ teaspoon salt
1 teaspoon baking powder
½ cup milk (I use 2% and it works well)
2 tablespoons anise hyssop leaves, chopped fine
1 tablespoon anise hyssop flowers, chopped fine
2 tablespoons lemon balm leaves, chopped fine
1 tablespoon mint leaves, chopped fine
½ cup unsalted butter, room temperature
1 cup granulated sugar
3 large eggs
1 teaspoon vanilla extract

Directions:

- Preheat an oven to 350 degrees F and butter and flour a 9 x 5 x 3-inch loaf pan.

- In a bowl, sift the flour with the salt and baking powder and set it aside.

- Pour the milk into small saucepan and place over medium heat. Let it get just warm and add the herbs. Cover with a plate or lid and let steep about 5 minutes.

- While the milk is cooling, beat the butter and sugar in a mixer bowl.

- Add the eggs, one at a time and mix until light and fluffy.

- Add the vanilla and mix in.

- Add some of the flour mixture alternately with the milk mixture. It is fine for the milk to be a little warm yet and do not strain out the herbs (leave them in). The milk should not be hot at all.

- When everything is well blended, pour the batter in the loaf pan and bake for about 45 minutes or until a toothpick inserted into the center comes out clean. The top should be golden and the edges should pull slightly away from the edge of the pan.

- Set the pan on a rack and cool for 10 minutes then turn out on a rack. Cut into slices and serve slightly warm or cold.

Old World German Potato Salad

Featuring: Caraway

One of my favorite things that my Grandmother used to make is German Potato Salad. It is vinegary and full of caraway seeds so it is also a little sweet. The recipe calls for fingerling potatoes, which are like the potatoes in Europe, but I have used red potatoes instead and was very happy with the dish. My grandmother would add some sugar to the potato salad and I never liked this much and would ask her to take my portion out before the addition. You may like the sweetness however, so give a try. This potato salad is served warm and is great on a cold winter night.

Ingredients:
1 tablespoon caraway seed
1 tablespoon Dijon mustard
¼ cup apple cider vinegar
¼ cup olive oil

salt and pepper to taste
1 pound fingerling potatoes, peeled if needed and cut into bite size pieces
¾ cup celery, chopped
¼ cup green onions, sliced thin
1 tablespoon granulated sugar, optional

Directions:

- In a bowl, whisk the caraway seed, mustard vinegar and olive oil. Add the salt and pepper and set aside.

- Bring a large pot of water to boil and add the potatoes. Cook about 15 minutes or until fork tender, but not soft. Drain and put in a bowl while still hot.

- Add the celery and green onions to the potatoes.

- If you are adding sugar, add it to the dressing and stir well to dissolve. It will completely dissolve when it comes in contact with the hot potatoes. Pour over and mix well.

- Serve warm.

Sweet and Lovely Cardamom Buns

Featuring: Cardamom

My aunt always served Cardamom Buns on St. Lucy's Day in December. It was part of her heritage and the oldest daughter in the house would bring the buns around in the morning singing a song and we would eat them and cold fruit soup with cheeses and meats. It was always a wonderful time. The buns were made by making ropes from the dough and curling them in a spiral above and below the middle. I don't always have time to do that so I make a rope and shape it in a figure eight. The recipe makes 12 buns.

Ingredients:
1 ¼ cup warm water at about 105 degrees F
¾ stick (6 tablespoons) unsalted butter, melted and cooled slightly

6 tablespoons granulated sugar
2 ¼ ounce package active dry years (about 4 ½ teaspoons)
3 large eggs, beaten slightly
1 teaspoon salt
¼ cup powdered nonfat dry milk
5 to 6 cups flour
¼ cup more unsalted butter, room temperature
½ cup more granulated sugar
2 tablespoons ground cinnamon
3 tablespoons cardamom seed, ground
egg wash (1 large egg with 2 tablespoons water mixed in)

Directions:

- In a bowl, pour in the water and take the temperature. When it reaches 105 degrees F, add the melted butter and sugar. Mix it up a bit and sprinkle the yeast over top. Let stand 5 minutes. It should get foamy.

- Using a wooden spoon, stir in the eggs, salt and dry milk.

- Add the flour 1 cup at a time until the dough becomes smooth and elastic. This will take some elbow grease and when it gets too hard, use your hands.

- Oil a bowl and place the dough in. Turn it to coat with oil and cover with plastic wrap.

- Place the bowl in a warm dry area to rise about 1 hour or until double.

- Place on a floured surface and punch down.

- Keep surface well-floured and roll with a rolling pin to a 15 by 25 inch rectangle. Spread the ¼ cup room temperature butter on top, sprinkle with sugar, cinnamon and cardamom.

- Roll like a jelly roll and cut 1 ½ inch slices. Place cut side down on parchment covered baking sheet about 2 inches apart or roll each slice into a rope and swirl into a figure 8 and place back on the parchment.

- Cover with a clean towel and let rise 1 hour.

- While rising, preheat the oven to 350 degrees F.

- Brush each bun with the egg wash and sprinkle on a little more sugar.

- Bake 25 minutes and remove to a cooling rack.

Sweet and Body Warming Potato Carrot Soup

Featuring: Cinnamon

The following recipe is incredible and it is also savory except for the sweetness of the sweet potato and carrots. Do not use baby carrots in this soup because you need a thicker texture of a full-grown carrot that has been peeled. This is a soup you might never think you will like, but if you try it, you will think differently especially because it is served either hot or cold. It is warming on a cold day or cooling during the heat of summer. Cinnamon slows down the rate at which the stomach digests food and evens out blood sugar as long as you don't add sugar to a recipe. This soup will fit the bill and it makes about 5 cups.

Ingredients:
2 cups sweet potato, peeled and chopped
2 cups carrots, peeled and chopped
1 ½ cups warm water
½ cup onion, peeled and chopped
¼ cup coconut oil
1 teaspoon ground cinnamon
¼ teaspoon ground cloves
¼ teaspoon ground nutmeg
¼ teaspoon ground allspice

Directions:
- Steam the chopped potatoes and carrots in a metal or bamboo steamer over hot water, or in an instant pot until they become tender.

- Place the steamed vegetables in a blender or food processor with the warm water and blend until it is smooth.

- Add onion, coconut oil, cinnamon, cloves, nutmeg and allspice and blend again until smooth and pour into a saucepan over low heat until heated through.

- Serve hot or let it cool, put in a covered container and place in the refrigerator overnight or at least 3 hours if you want to eat it cold.

Traditional Clove Studded Ham

Featuring: Cloves

The most beautiful hams I have seen are the ones that are studded with whole cloves. Cloves are a great anti-inflammatory spice and will make an upset stomach feel much better. Cloves have a rounded end and a sharp end and to stud the ham, you just poke the clove, sharp side down, into the surface of the ham. You can make designs or just stud the whole thing on the top and sides. The ham is cooked with the cloves in and they infuse flavor into the meat. In this recipe, a glaze is made and poured over the top of the studded ham. This recipe is for a 5 pound ham and it is delicious any time.

Ingredients:
5 pound fully cooked ham
¼ cup whole cloves
1 cup pineapple juice
1 cup brown sugar
½ cup honey
2 oranges, juiced

Directions:
- Preheat the oven to 350 degrees F.

- Place the ham in a roasting pan and stud the top with all the cloves. Just push them into the skin of the ham.

- Put the ham in the oven for about 20 minutes.

- Meanwhile, in a saucepan, put the pineapple juice, brown sugar, honey and the juice of the oranges. Place over medium high heat, stir and simmer about 10 minutes or until it thickens.

- Remove the ham from the oven and brush the glaze over the top and the cloves.

- Place the ham back in the oven for another 20 minutes and treat with glaze once more using all the glaze.

- Place in the oven another 10 to 15 minutes and remove. Let cool a few minutes and transfer to a cutting board.

- Remove all the cloves from the ham and slice.

Slow Cooker Chocolaty Chicken Mole

Featuring: Cocoa Powder

Everyone knows that chocolate improves mood and brain function, at least I know I feel better when I have chocolate. What you may not know is that it also makes blood vessels relax and therefore, may prevent heart attacks. (It is a good excuse to use cocoa powder). This recipe is for a mole sauce and chicken that is made in a slow cooker. It will definitely lift spirits around the dinner tables and makes 8 delicious servings.

Ingredients:
1 cup onions, peeled and chopped
1/3 cup golden raisins
1/3 cup dried currants
2 cloves garlic, peeled and minced
1 ½ teaspoon chili powder (I use ancho chili powder)
2 tablespoons toasted sesame seed
¾ teaspoon ground cumin
¾ teaspoon cinnamon
5 teaspoons cocoa powder
¼ teaspoon hot sauce
1 14.5-ounce can diced tomatoes
1 cup tomato sauce

1 cup chicken broth
3 pounds chicken breasts, boneless and skinless
¼ cup slivered almonds

Directions:

- Place the onions, raisins, currants, garlic, chili powder, sesame seeds, cumin, cinnamon, cocoa powder, hot sauce, tomatoes, tomato sauce and chicken broth in the bottom of a slow cooker and give it a stir.

- Add the chicken breasts and stir cover with the sauce.

- Cover and cook on low for 6 hours and turn to high another 3 hours or until the chicken is tender.

- Remove the chicken from the slow cooker and shred placing it back in the slow cooker.

- Heat it up and serve with sauce, sprinkling with almonds.

Festive Moroccan Couscous

Featuring: Coriander

Coriander is the seed of cilantro and it is good for digestion, colds and headaches. The following recipe has a bunch of ingredients, including coriander and many other spices, but it is well worth the trouble. The couscous is savory and sweet and makes 8 servings.

Ingredients:
1 ¼ teaspoon ground cumin
½ teaspoon ground ginger
¼ teaspoon ground cloves
1/8 teaspoon cayenne
½ teaspoon cardamom
½ teaspoon ground coriander
¼ teaspoon ground allspice
1 teaspoon olive oil
1 red onion, peeled and thinly sliced
1 red, green or yellow bell pepper, seeded and thin sliced

2 zucchinis, halved and cut in ¾ inch pieces
½ cup golden raisins
1 teaspoon sea salt
1 orange, just the zest
1 14.5-ounce can garbanzo beans (chickpeas) rinsed and drained
1 ½ cup chicken broth
½ cup orange juice (from the orange you zested)
1 ½ cup dry couscous
3 tablespoons fresh mint, chopped

Directions:

- In a small bowl, mix the cumin, ginger, cloves, cayenne, cardamom, coriander and allspice and whisk to combine.

- Place a large heavy pot over medium heat. Pour in the spice mix and stir while toasting until fragrant, about 2 to 3 minutes.

- Add the oil, onion, peppers and zucchini and stir for about 5 minutes.

- Stir in the raisins, salt, and orange zest.

- Add the broth and orange juice and stir to combine getting anything stuck to the pan up from the bottom. Bring to a boil.

- Remove from the heat and stir in the couscous. Cover a and let sit 5 minutes.

- Fluff with a fork and add the mint mixing until light, fluffy and well combined.

- Serve hot.

Zesty Ginger Beef Stir Fry

Featuring: Ginger

Ginger goes well with almost every Asian-inspired dish you can think of, but it goes especially well with beef. Normally I would say to not use ground ginger in a savory dish and always use a fresh finger with the skin peeled off and grated, but in this case powder form of ginger is used in the recipe, but fresh ginger cut in matchsticks is also used. The easy thing to remember is that powdered or candied ginger is mostly used in sweet dishes while fresh is mostly used in savory dishes. (There are always exceptions to this rule). This recipe is very easy to make and quick once the meat is done marinating and it makes 4 servings.

Ingredients:
2 tablespoons rice vinegar
5 tablespoons soy sauce
1 tablespoon honey
1 tablespoon ground ginger
1 teaspoon chili pepper flakes
1 teaspoon ground cumin
1 ½ pound top sirloin
1 tablespoon cornstarch
2 tablespoons vegetable oil
1 tablespoon dark sesame oil
3 green onions, sliced diagonally in thin slices
2 cloves garlic, peeled and sliced thin
1 inch nob ginger peeled and cut in matchsticks
½ cup cilantro, chopped

Directions:
- In a bowl, combine the rice vinegar, soy sauce, honey, ground ginger, pepper flakes and cumin. Mix well to make a thick marinade.

- Chill the top sirloin several hours before cooking. Slice it in thin strips. Soak the steak in the marinade covered for up to 4 hours in the refrigerator.

- Make a slurry in a bowl with the cornstarch and 2 tablespoons cold water.

- Heat a skillet or wok over medium high heat and add the vegetable oil and sesame oil. Let it get almost to smoking.

- Take the meat out of the marinade and dab off and place it in the wok, a handful at a time. Sauté to rare, about 1 minute and remove to an empty bowl.

- When the meat is done stir fry the onions and garlic about 45 sections. Add the beef back in and the slurry and stir constantly until everything thickens and is warm, about 2 minutes.

- Serve over hot rice.

Unusual but Delicious Licorice Beef Stew

Featuring: Licorice

The recipe chosen for this herb is interestingly good if you like licorice. It is for a beef stew that has that little oomph of something that might not be identified right away with some people, but those that love licorice will love it. Licorice goes well with the flavor of malt beer, but not so much with regular beer, so be sure to use a malt. The recipe calls for macerated prunes. Get dried prunes and soak them in either water, beef stock or some of the beer for about 1 hour to rehydrate and then use only the prunes and discard the liquid. This recipe makes 4 servings.

Ingredients:
2 pounds beef, trimmed and cut into bite size cubes
salt and pepper
2 yellow onions, peeled and chopped
2 carrots, peeled and chopped
2 ribs of celery, chopped
2 tablespoons butter
1/3 cup flour
1 clove garlic, peeled and smashed
1/3 cup balsamic vinegar
1 pinch red pepper flakes
7 ounces macerated prunes
4 bay leaves
4 sprigs fresh rosemary
4 inches, licorice root
3 ½ cups beef broth
3 cups malt beer
1 teaspoon sugar

Directions:

- Dry off the beef with paper towels and cut into cubes. Season with salt and pepper and put it in a bowl in the refrigerator 1 hour or overnight, covered.

- Chop the onion, carrots and celery and set aside.

- Heat the butter in a large Dutch oven over medium heat and sauté the garlic for about 2 minutes or until fragrant.

- Dredge the meat in the flour and brown the meat on all sides. Remove from the Dutch oven and set aside.

- Add the cut vegetables and sauté about 3 minutes.

- Add the vinegar and red pepper flakes and cook until the vinegar almost evaporates.

- Return the meat to the Dutch oven and add the prunes, bay leaves and rosemary.

- Throw in the licorice root and add the broth and the beer. Bring to a boil cover and simmer about 3 hours adding water if the liquid gets too low. When it is done, the meat should fall apart.

- Remove the bay leaves and licorice root. Add the sugar if needed and serve.

Spicy Holiday Drop Cookies

Featuring: Mace

The following recipe is an old one from a German woman I knew ages ago. The dough is rolled into balls and then rolled in sugar and baked. I use colored sugar even though the dough is dark from the molasses because it makes them glittery. I usually use lavender, pink, blue or green sugar and the recipe makes about 36 cookies. You can skip rolling them in sugar and instead, dust with powder sugar while warm for something different.

Ingredients:

¾ cup vegetable oil
¼ cup molasses
1 cup granulated sugar
2 large eggs
1 teaspoon vanilla
1 ¾ cup flour
1 cup whole wheat pastry flour
1 ½ teaspoon baking soda
½ teaspoon salt
1 ½ teaspoon ground cinnamon
1 ½ teaspoon ground ginger
1 teaspoon ground mace
2 teaspoons ground cloves
½ cup colored sugar (optional)

Directions:

- In a large bowl, whisk the oil with the molasses until well combined.

- Add the sugar, eggs and vanilla and mix well.

- In another bowl combine the flour, wheat pastry flour, baking soda, salt, ground cinnamon, ground ginger, ground mace and ground cloves and whisk.

- Use a wooden spoon and elbow grease to combine the dry ingredients into the wet ingredients gradually. Once combined form dough into a ball, place in the bowl, cover with plastic wrap and put in the refrigerator overnight.

- Preheat the oven to 350 degrees F and prepare a baking sheet with parchment paper.

- Place the colored sugar in a bowl.

- Make 1 ½ inch balls from the chilled dough, roll in sugar and place on baking sheets about 2 inches apart.

- Bake 10 to 12 minutes or until the tops darken.

- Cool 5 minutes on the baking sheet and remove to cooling racks.